CHRONICLES of Deplorabella

DEPLORABELLA

Copyright © 2025 by Deplorabella

All rights reserved.

ISBN: 978-1-962768-14-6

No part of this publication may be reproduced, distributed, or transmitted in any form or by any means, including photocopying, recording, or other electronic or mechanical methods, without the prior written permission of the publisher or author, except as permitted by U.S. copyright law. For permission requests, contact info@oceannapolis.com.

Published by Oceannapolis, LLC

https://oceannapolis.com

Book Cover Design by 100 Covers

This book is dedicated to my supportive family

CONTENTS

1.	OPENING SHOT	1
2.	MODEST BEGINNINGS	9
3.	BROKEN NOSE, BROKEN PROMISES	18
4.	TRAUMA	27
5.	BITTER CANYON	35
6.	ON MY TOES	42
7.	SOVIET INSANITY	47
8.	HARD TO FOLLOW	52
9.	SEEING THROUGH THE LIES	58
10.	CRYING FOR THEM AND ME	64
11.	LEGACY	72
12.	BABY TEETH	80
13.	MEMORIES BEYOND A LIFETIME	87
14.	LEN, MY LOVE	94
15.	SEA CHANGES	102
16.	WESTERN SKIES	114

17. WILDLIFE	121
18. WARNINGS AND HISTORY	124
19. PRODUCTIONS AND IMPRESSIONS	130
20. FRIENDSHIPS THROUGH THE YEARS	137
21. CAREER TALES AND ANECDOTES	144
22. DEVOTED PROFESSIONAL	152
23. JUST DESSERTS AND MEMORIES	159
24. FALMOUTH, FULL CIRCLE	167
ACKNOWLEDGEMENTS	173
READ MORE	174
ABOUT THE AUTHOR	175

1

OPENING SHOT

The summer I was ten, I thought I could still be saved from...

The summer season carried a false promise. It started in the usual way, at the end of the school year when the streets became our playground. But inside the house, at any moment, for any reason, my mother, Frances, could scream at us. We had not cleaned the bathroom well enough, and "the corners!" she shrieked. "Do not neglect the corners." She warned that we did not scrub the plates quite clean. One of us had a fresh mouth.

We did not live in a television sitcom awaiting the arrival of the "father who knew best." My mother greeted him with a litany of grievances against her children. She incited Victor to slam into the room I shared with my sister, Tina, or to throw open the door to my brother Eddie's room. Victor beat us. He was serious about punishment. Once, he broke his thumb while smashing Tina's head against the wall. It was all in a day's work.

Victor smoked cigarettes, cigars, and pipes. Cigarettes were the staple that we did not associate with any particular mood or behavior. But the cigar and pipe were different. Smoking one, he became mellow and resisted my mother's mounting demands that he deal with us. Smoking the other, he became more volatile, puffing smoke like a smoldering volcano. Then he erupted with curses and howls while trapping us in terror. I used to know which smoke was which before the exact memory faded in a cloud of haze.

My mother figured out how to extract retribution for having robbed her of her life without having to administer the beatings herself. All she had to do was set him off. She did so with more statistical reliability than NASA later demonstrated launching rocket ships into space.

Along with my sister, Tina, and my brother, Eddie, I shared in common some of the relics and rituals of childhood with the more fortunate kids. We eventually got bicycles when we moved out of a one-bedroom apartment in New York City. We also got a dog and birthday cakes that seemed to make our childhoods indistinguishable from that of our neighbors. Appearances could deceive an outsider.

The father who watched television in his red-checked bathrobe touched himself while my siblings and I were in the room. We spent a lot of time huddling in the closet in our room. We comforted each other after a beating or knowing we were in trouble, and we anticipated his jackbooted assault on the steps and the ear-shattering sound of a door flung open. I never thought I would make it to age twenty-one.

As victims of dysfunctional families, we might have fallen into despair and considered suicide. We could not envision life beyond what we knew. Lacking perspective, we might have succumbed to the seduction of ending the torment by ending our lives. We would also have ended our prospects beyond our hellish home life. Fantasies of making people sorry for how they treated us would have faded along with the memorial tributes to us. We might have sought refuge, even as adults, in alcohol or drugs. Somehow, we realized that hurting yourself never provided the answer to other people hurting you.

We escaped, branded with fear. Nightmares held us hostage for decades. We discovered many children who carried their closets around. Burdened into adulthood, they turned later to therapy or AA to replenish the deleted inner resources required to live their lives. Hunched in the closet, I hoped my parents would vanish. I did not want to assume responsibility for wishing them dead. I just wanted them to be gone.

I wished Tina, Eddie, and I could move in with my favorite Aunt Gail in

Boston. She was not at all like my mother, which qualified her eminently for the role of mother and Guardian Angel aunt. Her daughters, ten and twelve years older than me, grew up in a glamorous landscape of white luggage and scented stationery on which they wrote their boyfriends. They had their own bathroom and closets filled with cocktail dresses. A music box played "La Vie en Rose." Bookshelves offered Al Capp's hillbilly heaven of Dogpatch. Bottles of perfume lined up on their dressing tables. They were the recipients of Gail's hard-scrabble life in which she rose from poverty to a judgeship in Democrat-controlled Boston. All of us enjoyed being the beneficiaries of her generous and loving spirit.

When we visited her mansion, I believed everything was possible. I would crawl into her bed early in the morning and ask her to tell me about the world. Each time she regaled me with stories about another country, she would point to the globe with her polished fingernail. I would listen, warmed by the covers, her smile, and her firsthand knowledge of the whole wide world.

When they stopped at our North Jersey house, driving back from Florida, Aunt Gail and Uncle Carl arrived bearing gifts. They delivered jars of orange marmalade, baskets of ripe fruit, and invitations to eat at a local "fancy restaurant" we never frequented without them. Years later, my husband Len and I returned to that location to host two parties. The first welcomed our older son Seth back from a deployment to Iraq. The second celebrated the three spring birthdays of my husband and both sons. This time, we were the hosts welcoming a hundred or more friends and family. I never thought it was possible. I had to live long enough to find out it was possible.

Time spent with Aunt Gail transfused the joy that kept me going. One weekend, she invited me to stay at the Park Sheraton Hotel in NYC. They took me to a restaurant. I saw a comedy, *A Funny Thing Happened on the Way to the Forum*, with Phil Silvers. I accompanied their stylish family of four to the pier where my cousins, Ida and Marion, toting white luggage, purchased gum for their cruise to Europe. They bought Clorets gum for fifteen cents, three times the cost of an ordinary pack. My family met us at the dock to take me home when Gail and her family boarded.

While my relatives sailed to Europe, I returned to the other side of the Hudson where my mother handed me a broom. "You can forget about all of that. You're home now," she said. Until I retired, I regarded every address as a place to work, not a home in which to live.

My love of travel and the necessity of vacations are attributable in part to the time spent with my aunt. As an adult, I satisfied some of my curiosity about the world with books. I refused to visit countries hostile to our own and remained wary of the Potemkin Village overview offered by many tours. I never imagined cruising almost two dozen times or visiting almost half of our 63 American national parks. My husband turned my aunt's tales into trips.

Music transported me far away from the household chores I performed. Songs taught me that time spent raising my own family made my house a place of cheer rather than a site of indentured servitude. The time lag between an outdated outlook and a new and improved perspective indicated that I beat myself up long after my father stopped beating me. Music helped me make an attitude correction to an increasingly harmonious reality.

I did not know the term "defining moment," even when it hit me. Hurricane Carol hit the northeast, slamming into my chronology. Events before Carol became a type of BC on my calendar. AD meant after the deaths of five family members.

I had already been introduced to disease and death. One night, my father talked about his own father's death from a bleed in the brain. Then my mother explained how a cousin deprived of oxygen was disabled at birth. From then on, I was squeamish, passing out with regularity in junior and senior high. I got woozy and slid off a lab stool at the mere mention of a leech. I could dissect a frog in biology class but could not handle the conversations. In college, I had to lower my head between my knees when I found myself at a meal with a bunch of bio majors. They had no difficulty exchanging scalpels for forks while recounting their discoveries.

Anyway, after that summer, childhood continued to be what it had been. Except that the next summer, there was no longer a beach house for a vacation in Cape Cod. The near future held no prospect of escape from my parents.

I remain a baby who cannot watch the predator hunt down and eat his prey on the nature shows, even though I know the lion cubs need food. Having my own children forced me to learn more about blood, diseases, and operations than I ever wanted to know.

Life is always teaching us lessons in humility. Some lessons happen to make me pass out.

When Eddie, Tina, and I asked our mother if the two aunts and three cousins could ever be brought back to life, she said, "maybe." She answered noncommittally despite knowing that their bodies had washed up along the bay and could never breathe again. She went to the funerals alone. Dark-eyed Pamela, smiling Edith, and toddler Norman, so alive during our week with them, were lowered into graves I never got to visit.

No one ever talked to us about our feelings. We had to move our cousins, very much alive on our recent visit, from the ranks of the living to the dead. We were free to imagine their terror, screams, a rising sea level, drowning, the roof blowing off, walls knocked down, and bones broken on the rocks along the shore. The house and all it held were gone.

God and religion did not exist in my parents' house. Neither did the Easter Bunny nor Santa Claus. We did not play with dreidels or have any semblance of religious tradition or instruction. Scripture came from *The Communist Manifesto*, not the Old and New Testaments. No illusions survived in this grim fairy tale. My mother insisted on Marxist proselytizing at extended family get-togethers. She made herself a pariah, so we were deprived of contact with culture and cousins. Invitations to religious celebrations ended.

In college, I traveled the NY subways to Brooklyn and the Bronx with Len, my boyfriend and eventual husband who introduced me to a world more normal and more Jewish. At my first seders, his relatives debated the merits of "sinkers" and "floaters" when it came to matzoh balls at his aunt's or his grandmother's. They took special care to welcome in the holidays with prayer and songs. The songs recited ancient suffering and showed fidelity to faith. Our sons benefitted from their spiritual and culinary legacy, something for which I hungered without giving it a name…until Len entered my life.

In the aftermath of Hurricane Carol, I had no glimpse of a future role in a Jewish if not particularly observant home. I once announced that no son of mine would ever have a Bar Mitzvah. That was only one of many declarations I later denounced. Seth and Jake astounded me with their mastery of Judaism required for their participation in the ceremonies. They continued to delight me with their deep affinity for their faith. I thank Len for his forbearance during my years of professional atheism, a twisted offshoot of my inherited communism. It seemed I ingested too much propaganda in my pablum.

One year before the storm, another harbinger of tragedy arrived. Sewer gas overcame my Uncle Milton and Grandpa Manny while they tried to repair a disposal in a new house. As our extended family shrunk, my parents' horrific behavior and indoctrination worsened. My mother was one of five sisters. Until she died at 88, she had one passion, communism. It cost us our extended family. I realized in retrospect it cost us faith in God, though not forever…

I reached my 50s before I reconnected with some of the strangers who were cousins in my extended family. I never met "the wealthy" cousins who periodically shipped cartons of outgrown clothes. Reliant on hand-me-downs, I never cultivated a sense of style or made selections according to my tastes. Tina, despite the same experiences, managed to develop a predictably unique design sense based on her artistic talents.

I discovered recently that I had several things in common with my mother. We both dismissed clothes as superficial, an act of ideological denial. We were amateur actresses. We both loved Grieg's compositions. We both had osteoporosis. I preferred to think I shared more with my aunts, particularly two of her four sisters. My mother loved her oldest sister Gail but hated her youngster sister Ann. She shut me off from both of them, the two of her sisters I loved most. One was a victim of Hurricane Carol. The other, rarely accessible to me, suffered from my mother's jealousy.

My parents kept many secrets, but they told us things they should not have, trying to poison us against their "counterrevolutionary" relatives. She hated Ann because she was incredibly beautiful, enjoyed a professional career singing opera, and was their mother's favorite. My grandmother, Naomi, was a difficult woman. She once threw a knife at Frances and happily shipped her off to one of her sisters to live for a time. For my rejected mother, hatred of Ann was envy, as green as jade.

Twice I dressed in an outfit sent by distant cousins who lived within hours of us in New Jersey. Once, dressed in a plaid-pleated skirt with the refrain repeated on the cuffs, collar, and covered buttons on a black velvet jacket, I went to see Ann perform. I wore it accompanying my mother by bus and subway to the City Center Opera where Ann's soprano established its hegemony over the hall. I had begged and nagged for months to see her.

Aunt Ann was a bright red balloon drifting above the trees. My hold on her was no more than a string I held in my hand. My mother made me let go. She resented any access I had to her, so encounters were few. Strains of *Carmen* and *La Boheme* faded. It took me decades to reclaim my aunt and the music. Of my mother's four sisters, two became my favorites not only because they were wonderful but because my mother's intermittent permission for me to love them never diminished that attachment.

My Aunt Gail survived poverty and a mother as indifferent as a blue sky over Auschwitz to become a judge. She worked her way through law school in a cookie factory. Her pantry rivaled the supermarket shelves, lined with every kind of cookie and breakfast cereal imaginable. Even the fragrant roses in her garden seemed to be sugar-sprinkled. On a glass table in a spare bedroom, she arranged clusters of jars of nail polish. It was a greenhouse blooming with liquid blossoms, cherry, crimson, vermilion, and scarlet. She started with nothing but her own dreams. Having realized them, she concentrated on making all her family members happy.

As a child, I thought I was looking at the perfect home. A driveway followed the rise past the mansion to a separate multicar garage around the back. Brightly striped awnings and the grandeur of the entry promised a world of relative luxury. On one side, opening to the double living rooms, one spacious formal room showcased a grand piano. The other, less formal living room, featured seating around a television set. A separate bar boasted big glass windows and fishnets draped below the ceiling. Bright glass swizzle sticks, glasses of all sizes, and mermaids affixed to the walls made the bar a magical place.

On the other side of the house was a large glass-enclosed room, later converted into a playroom. The house featured several bathrooms as well as a first-floor powder room, large fish tanks, and a formal dining room. A pantry with fine dinnerware and board games like Scrabble separated the dining room from a large kitchen. The upstairs hallway overlooked the stairs and entries to several rooms. A second-floor nook had a built-in desk and a chair drawn up to provide an office for Uncle Carl.

My Aunt Gail's husband brought home bags of salted pistachio nuts and assorted licorice candies for us to nibble while watching television. The uncle who rearranged his comb-over, to pretend to be a monster, chased us shrieking up and down the stairs. He also played songs from *Victory at Sea* and *Lilly* on the piano. Years later, I found out he was a philanderer. He went out to tryst the evening Gail fell down the stairs and suffered a miscarriage.

Carl and Gail's house was paradise for us. It was something less for the woman who lived there. Perhaps he never forgave his wife for having become a judge while he remained a lawyer. She remained a faithful, loving wife. He was repeatedly more casual about his vows. I still hold to earlier memories of a beloved, fun-loving uncle. Later realizations did not abrogate the earlier ones. My uncle taught me that a person can be multifaceted. Later assessments reflected a more cynical acknowledgement. They also pivoted me to a more profound love and respect for my aunt. She endured despite all the heartbreak, and she offered her loving hospitality to all her relatives.

2

MODEST BEGINNINGS

My family started out in a tiny apartment in Washington Heights. We moved out rather than up to a succession of modest, older houses in blue-collar suburban towns. Whenever a mouse showed up in the kitchen, my mother left. She hated mice and there was no room for an uninvited guest.

My parents prized their privacy while disrespecting ours. They never wanted to have room for visitors who would inhibit their behavior. We begged for company, hoping to mitigate the dynamics. On a handful of occasions Aunt Ann's older son, Paul, was allowed to come for a weekend in the summer. That meant a trip to Lake Sebago or Lake Welch, pizza at a local tavern, a movie at the 303 Drive In, and lots of time for us to play tricks on each other and just have fun. Paul joined Eddie and Tina in planting cups of water above the door, hoping that when I opened it, the movement would send the cups crashing down to surprise and soak me. It never worked, but they never stopped trying. I never stopped laughing.

In New Jersey, we were always odd man out. Surrounded by kids from parochial school, we had to run home fast to escape our tormentors. Unfortunately, we didn't run fast enough. Eddie sustained several concussions. I imagined taking lunar leaps high above the danger gravity condemned me to.

I could not even imagine any superman trait that would protect me from my parents on the other side of the door. Yeah, the neighborhood kids were ball-breakers who always had pennies for jawbreakers. We never received an allowance. We rarely pocketed change for gum or candy, but I ended up with lots of cavities anyway.

Remembering is like looking into a kaleidoscope. New configurations keep changing, interrupting the narrative, shutting down light and shadow, and propelling shards of reflected color.

Tragedy struck a year before the hurricane. Another of my mother's sisters, my Aunt Miriam, moved with her family. She married an engineer who was in love with her sister, Ann. He married Miriam on the rebound. The less than happily married couple would never live happily ever after in their new home in a new Massachusetts suburban development. We visited, impressed by the fancy new design, a split-level. It was not the small, old, up-and-down kind with a bleak, moldy basement like we always had.

My cousins had brand new blonde wood furniture and huge piggy banks filled with coins we inherited when the cousins drowned the following summer. But this year before Falmouth, they were still very alive. They met new neighborhood friends who had hammocks in their backyards. They wore their hair plaited in long braids and sported penny loafers. Tina and I had to wear the ugly brown Oxfords our mother insisted were better for our feet. I had already started ballet and pointe lessons early and ended up with crooked toes and bunions. I still love saddle shoes and lust for penny loafers.

Horror seemed to stalk our summer visits. When the brand-new garbage disposal clogged, my Uncle Milton and Grandfather Manny tried to fix it. Sewer gas overcame them. Even the firemen called to rescue them from the ditch barely escaped asphyxiation. That marked the end of the model home in the model development. Aunt Miriam lost her husband. Her little children lost their father. They moved in with everybody's favorite aunt, Aunt Gail. Our fantasy of living with her became our cousins' reality, imposed on them by tragedy and loss.

Someone found a letter written by the seven-year-old Pamela before she died. She had written her dead father and hidden the letter in a book. She was deeply unhappy. She knew her parents favored her five-year-old always smiling sister

Edith and baby brother, Norman. She had long, beautiful black eyelashes. She played Scrabble extraordinarily well. She knew lots of big words to describe her big sorrow. On the game board, the big words earned her points.

After our visit the following summer, they were all gone. The lettered tiles disappeared into the waves. The letter was later retrieved from a book in Gail and Carl's mansion. Aunts Gail and Miriam were dead along with her three little children. Gone....

Upon retiring, Len and I moved into the first of two model homes in two model developments. We still play Scrabble with our sons and grandson.

Once my widowed aunt Miriam and her three children moved into Gail's mansion, the judge and her husband, my Uncle Carl, bought a beach house on Cape Cod. Miriam's family would spend the entire summer there along with our grandmother. Gail and Carl spent weekends at the Cape. Other sisters and their families were invited to musical chair vacations throughout the course of the summer. Vacations were idyllic.

My grandmother Naomi was widowed again when her husband inhaled sewer gas. My grandfather, whom I knew, used to climb Florida palm trees to gather coconuts for us. I can still see him, wiry, good-natured and loving. When my grandmother lost him, it was one more loss in a long life of mourning. She married repeatedly throughout her many years. She outlived her husbands. Then she outlived her children.

During the summer of 1954, my cousins had bikini bathing suits and water shoes to protect their feet from pebbles on the beach. They had their own first floor bedrooms while visiting cousins camped out on mattresses in a loft. You had to pull a rope to lower a ladder to get down to the bathroom or use the chamber pots provided in the loft. My grandmother spent the summer in mourning, making cheese blintzes and watching Pinkie Lee and Kate Smith on television. A picket fence surrounded a mongrel yard, part sand, part beach grasses. Auntie Gail would commute from Boston each weekend to coax roses to grow along the salt-encrusted trellises. Paradise was a swing set in the backyard and a ladder down to the private beach.

We kids crawled like snails into empty shells, enjoying big black inner tubes as shiny as patent leather stationed in the surf. Uncle Carl parked his speed boat on the ramp. He took relays of cousins five miles out to fish. On my turn, someone caught a blowfish. We watched it puff itself into importance. We watched my uncle cut it down to size for bait. On Tina's turn, she caught a sand shark. Uncle Carl used an oar to club the shark into obedience and cut it loose. Just the speed of the boat, the slap of the waves on the sides, the sting of the salt in our eyes, the warmth of the sun on our skin…it would never end.

When someone tried to convince my grandmother to go out to dinner, or go dancing, or do something she used to enjoy she would dismiss the very idea. "It would be like dancing on seven graves." When someone tried to convince my mother to devote more time to her pottery or painting, hobbies she enjoyed and for which she displayed some talent, she would dismiss the very idea. "It would be putting myself before the revolution." She spent her last decades churning out tomes of Stalinist propaganda for Canadian communist publishers when she could have enjoyed life and artistic productivity. I never read her books. By then I had had a lifetime of her articles, lectures, and ultimatums.

My grandmother and mother were both martyrs to unrelenting, irrepressible grief. They locked out life, light, and love. They failed to shut out despair. Instead, they wrapped themselves in a permanent chrysalis of pain, never to emerge as creatures of beauty.

Subsequent summer vacations usually translated into a day trip or two. We might take the train or ferry to Bear Mountain to escape the heat of Hillside Avenue. Once we moved to Jersey, it meant a picnic at a state park with a lake, or a day at the Bear Mountain swimming pool. Most days we played outside, treasuring the carefree hours between cold cereal breakfast and overcooked hot supper. Infrequently, my mother provided coins for a Good Humor purchase from the truck.

Here is what other families did. Lots of them went down the Jersey Shore for a week or two. They rented a little bungalow blocks off the beach, grilled meat, and walked boardwalks. They ate salt-water taffy, rode amusement park rides, and gorged on cones of swirling custard. They played in the sea, learning how to jump the crest of a wave or swim underneath it.

Some families went to a campsite, a cabin, or a hotel in the mountains. They saw shows and ordered plates and plates of food they did not have to finish but could if they wanted to. They swam in chilly lakes or chlorinated pools. They played camp games like color wars or participated in planned activities.

Other families stayed home. The kids swung back and forth in their backyard swings or at local parks. They read comic books in a tree house or a fort in the basement. On weekends they might go to the local movie theater for the double feature, cartoon, newsreel, and serial. They could stay and watch it again when it ended while temperatures soared outside as showings were continuous. They ate frozen fruit juice pops from their freezer, or with a pocketful of change they picked from the portable treasures of the Good Humor truck or Bungalow Bar, which announced its arrival with a jingle.

Here is what my family did. Eddie, Tina, and I had chalk, a Spaulding ball, bicycles, roller skates and a skate key hanging on a rope from my neck. We played dodge ball in the schoolyard until our parents called us home to dinner at six, one hour after everyone else had gone. Preparing children to be non-conformists promotes a commendable goal within reason. Our father, Victor, wore a beret and rode his bicycle downtown to pick up the NY Times. We could not have a high school jacket, but we were well versed in all the books of our family library. Each jacket contained a Marxist title or displayed a communist author.

Our path to non-conformity did not skirt the intellectual gulag. No dissidents contaminated their bookshelves or their consciousness. We read books that passed the test of socialist realism. We practiced a dogmatic non-conformity our parents dictated. The ways in which we resembled our peers and the ways in which we differed were not of our choosing. Every act of autonomous rebellion amounted to an act of counterrevolution. Our parents enacted scenes of warfare throughout our adolescence against our rebellion.

Our dog had endless litters of puppies. We pushed them around in doll carriages until they were weaned on pablum and we gave them to neighbors. We repeated the puppy pattern the summer of 1954. We found homes for all the puppies while we waited expectantly for our week at the Cape. Our parents would not be able to yell at us or beat us the whole time we were there. It was only a week. I thought it lasted forever.

Sometimes, when I drove home from work years later, I would suddenly smell the sea the way it filled my lungs that summer in Cape Cod. I found pieces of coke bottle, no longer sharp, but smooth. Opaque souvenirs of sea glass colored my matte memories. We cousins harvested sea-sculpted jewels on our beach. Today I have conch shells filled with grey-green gems my sons and grandson found years later while exploring other beaches.

Sometimes, I cast music like a net into the waves of memory and dredged up the tunes and lyrics of 1954. I taught my brother and sister and three little cousins as many of the words to "Back in Your Own Backyard" as I could retrieve. Mornings we crossed the street to the bay and danced around the sand dunes. I choreographed a musical show we performed on the swing set for all the adults.

One of Gail's daughters, the glamorous blonde Marion, who majored in French at Wellesley visited long enough to teach Tina and me the lyrics to an operatic aria in French. A few nights ago, we reprised our duet on a telephone call. Music thrives in memory when much else is lost. Maybe that began my love affair with the French language, which I studied in high school and college. I note with dismay the reluctantly accelerated, age-induced obliteration of a language I have not used recently except for encountering Haitians in an ER room who needed translation.

I did conduct much of the research for my MA thesis on the French Revolution in the language that pronounced words of terror and totalitarianism with such elegance. The literary and historical rapid transit took the nation of France from salon society expressing elevated principles to suppliers of an insatiable guillotine.

The French infatuation with communism, the fatal flaw of its Enlightenment philosophes and contemporary philosophers, continues, as does my love of the language. I recognize the truth in Shaw's musical translation of *My Fair Lady*, "The French don't care what they do so much if they pronounce it properly."

For no discernible reason, I would smell the cotton candy that permeated the carnival that Gail took us to one night. I could taste the Sugar Daddy I was working on when I lost a baby tooth standing waist-deep in the surf at a public beach in Falmouth. I would look at the older girls, the teenagers, and think I would never have a body like that. And I never did.

Memories like newly minted pennies keep showing up, dropped on the shore by a spendthrift tide. I teach all the kids the tinker toy pieces of songs. I choreograph dances and wait for truth like a yellow Tonka truck to drive up. Then, it's showtime, and the adults occupy picnic table benches, warming themselves with blankets. The black ocean spits salt at the delicate flowers planted around the house. The grownups sit like parishioners, prepared to be quiet, content to wait, already filled with dinner and grace. A punctual pale white moon, thin as a sacramental wafer, arrives uninvited. The show is a success. No one falls from the monkey bars or gets hit by a swing.

Mere weeks later I play dodge ball with friends in the school yard after another inedible dinner the three of us feed secretly to the overweight dog waiting beneath the kitchen table. In grade school a classmate nicknames me "Fossil." I am back home waiting for another box of secondhand clothes from a rich cousin on my mother's side whom I never meet. I await the opening of school and the first day of sixth grade. Now it is time. The beginning of a new school year, an 11th birthday on the horizon, and the end of innocent childhood illusions awaits.

The hurricane causes the sea and bay to rise, cover the thin road of separation and meet in an inescapable expanse of seething waters. It causes a tidal wave that makes the house disappear. A human chain cannot reach them. A mountain of water obliterates sand dunes and sun. They are all dead, like the stingray. They wash up days later, driftwood deposited on the edge of morning.

Phone calls go back and forth between New Jersey, Falmouth, and Boston.

The surviving family members call evacuation centers with urgency and desperation shaping their inquiries. They are not there. My aunts' bodies appear first. My mother tells her sister Ann that if the children survive, she will take them. Then, I do not know what to wish for my cousins. It does not matter, though, as their bodies appear. The last remains of the smiling five-year-old wash up battered against the rocks. They are all gone and my life has never been the same.

Childhood fractured, like music fierce yet perishable, banished to silence by the shafts of morning light. Death is inescapable. My own death is inescapable. Decades of nightmares begin. Tides rise faster than people can heed my calls to evacuate the beaches. I try to rescue my cousins, my sister and brother, and later my sons. The tidal wave swallows the beach, the distance between danger and safety, death and escape. Finally, a few years ago, I woke myself one night crying out, "Why do I have to be the one to save them?"

Because no one told me anything, I imagined everything.

I consider the sheer terror for the adults knowing they could not save the children. The horror for the children knowing the adults could not save them!

Later I read Elie Weisel's *Night*, in which he recounted his journey through the hellish landscape of the Holocaust with his child's hand deposited in his father's hand. Both realized that his father was unable to rescue him. Elie, a sensitive child, envisioned his father's despair knowing that his son knew they were completely vulnerable.

You never totally vanquish the vampiric memories of man's inhumanity, but you do find purpose in sharing the tales of survival. You honor the spirit of hope that enables the wounded to welcome their own children into a life without guarantees. The three of us were not included in the communal mourning. We did not attend the funeral. Nobody discussed our feelings or fears with us. Our parents held out hands to hit us, not to offer consolation.

We knew then that death could take even the young. Death could churn up the coast after our family. It could follow upon any visit we made to unsuspecting relatives. Cousins could die or be taken from us by storms of nature or of family politics. We could all die.

My brother is gone now. My sister and I would talk about that summer when I balanced on the last ledge of ten before toppling into a time when I was no longer a child but not yet a teenager. We cry.

For decades, I did not live one week without remembering my relatives murdered by the hurricane. I continued to wonder what would have become of them had they lived.

They continue in my thoughts today.

I am aware of the endless cycles of repetition and the tides of blood and salt. Their faces never faded like sepia photographs. I can still see them clearly. The hurricane of loss still churns.

3

BROKEN NOSE, BROKEN PROMISES

On a night when the moon revealed a scab of light in a cobalt sky, I tried to pawn my past. I held a photo of my red-haired baby sister, my curly-haired brother and me in a circlet of blond curls. The photographer dressed us in costumes of colorful gypsy scarves and bits of ribbon. Our parents' disappointment would not be visible in the professional poses. The photo triggered insomniac insights that slipped downstairs like a slinky toy at dawn's intrusion. I scraped a messy residue from the pot of memory. My brother's death did not come any more easily than his life.

If a book of Genesis existed to illuminate the victims of bullies, my brother would be inscribed. Our father, famous for winning debates by decibel level, roared him through multiplication tables. He growled him past grammar and pummeled him past spelling. Eddie was born with a lazy eye and wore a pirate-style patch that would start a trend today. Unusual at the time, it triggered suspicion. He suffered from schizophrenia. Years of therapy and drug treatment gave him some semblance of a normal life.

He progressed from elementary school failures to high school and college academic successes. An embittered, belligerent man who called himself his father motivated Eddie to earn good grades. He never recovered from the failure he was judged to be.

"Not the head, Victor, not the head," our mother would admonish her mate while he administered his two-fisted tutorials. He spit epithets like "faggot" and "idiot" to red pencil every wrong answer my brother gave. What epithets had the power to convey Victor's failure as a father?

Our mother mastered the knack of maneuvering our father to administer punishment without getting her hands dirty. She could also convince herself of her compassion when she called him off. She lit the fuse and feigned innocence. When he turned on her, we were all out of the house and there was no one left to call him off in faraway California.

My father bullied Eddie inside the house without remorse. His paternal concern extended only to bullies outside the house. He knew he could purchase no lasting peace with neighboring kids who perched like vultures on branches of a tree overhanging our yard. They watched Eddie and attacked him on the street. They made him lose consciousness without dirtying their parochial school uniforms. My father staged short intervals of truce by throwing an occasional backyard barbecue. He fed those kids sizzling hot dogs and hamburgers, satisfying their craving for raw meat for a time.

Our parents took us hiking through the once-upon-a-time woods of Englewood Cliffs. Long ago, trees were felled to clear space for pricey homes. My father called me back so that my brother could lead. It made sense to give the boy always under assault at school and in the streets a chance to shine. He might have explained his reasoning to me, but we were never entitled to explanations. We probably missed a few lessons they might have conveyed. We were not worthy of words when beatings would do. We thought they would never end, but they did.

The three of us went on to hike far from home through cool layered canopies of forest and into sun-spackled glades of wonder. Tina and I outlived the need to co-exist with our paternal guide who might well have led the doomed hikers to the Donner Pass. Eddie escaped to Ohio parks that were parent-free before cancer caught up to him at the end of the trail.

While living in a small house in a hostile neighborhood, we endured parental separation and a pagan version of Christmas. Every year we had the tree and presents that our communist parents somehow determined were appropriate. One year Eddie got an electric train set. Gift giving was rare. I usually declined any offer to pick out a toy on the grounds that they could not afford to buy me anything. I got credit for self-denial and showing awareness of our financial straits. A rejection of materialism and repudiation of consumption won me a temporary reprieve from their displeasure.

Good grades, reciting the communist credo, and disavowing any need for discretionary purchases won me approval. It was always conditional. I understood that. None of the money I earned in summer jobs turned out to be discretionary. It defrayed the costs of college along with campus jobs and loans. I understood the need for frugality. If only I could have escaped their threats when I escaped the closet and fled to college, seeking refuge. It was not money I needed. It was peace. That would come later, much later than it needed to. Renouncing communism for my Jewish heritage gave me that peace. I had to claim my escape routes to follow them.

One year our parents fought about money for a bicycle for Eddie. Our father ate lunch every weekday in an expensive restaurant. He enjoyed a couple of vodka gimlets and sometimes treated a colleague. There was no money left for the bike. He was very competitive, always jumping into a pool before our Uncle Michael, Ann's husband, to race him to the other side. Our uncle never knew a race was in progress. Victor could execute a cartwheel on ice skates and jump on a pogo stick. He could fence and shoot arrows into a target placed in a tree in the backyard. He obviously resented his son's inability to win the glory that eluded him. Pride and the Communist Party were his cruel masters.

Feeling cheated by life, he treated himself to fine dining and drinking. Our manipulative mother too felt cheated by life, but martyrdom was more her style.

As it happened, my brother could ride a bicycle for 30 or 40 miles, swim and water ski for hours. The patch discarded, his weak eye strengthened. His spine and muscles grew straight and strong, but his soul remained bent by abuse. Our mother, fed up with her husband's self-indulgence and refusal to buy the bike, left home for refuge in her sister Gail's house in Boston. The three of us spent a solemn Christmas holiday while our father sat around smoking, waiting for the phone to ring or not.

Years later I saw him smack her hard in their final, more upscale house in Jersey. She decorated the kitchen with a whimsical horoscope she painted on the walls, just below the ceiling. Neither astrology nor astronomy saved her from a constellation of family chaos. Later she took out a restraining order against him, charging him with spousal abuse. Her horoscope sign was the hammer and sickle.

They finished their lives in toney La Jolla, emptying their bank accounts into separate addresses.

My grandmother left my mother money and instructions to give portions of the inheritance to the three of us and other cousins as well. My mother never did. When he died my father was left with at least $100,000. He bequeathed my grandmother's legacy to his lawyer, a "dirty capitalist" of Marxist orthodoxy. He disinherited his two remaining children and three grandchildren.

It constituted the final beatdown he administered with his will. Fortunately, Len sent him a letter in which he praised our son, his grandson, for his enlistment in the U.S. Army and contrasted his patriotism with his grandfather's treasonous affinity for communism. I hope it forced him to confront an ideology bereft of humanity and a life lived without meaning.

My mother once confided that when I was twelve, she asked me for permission to divorce him. She said I had given her the okay. She returned from Boston before the tree was dismantled or the decorations were put away. She never divorced him. She just waited out the decades and died. She never found "the Age of Aquarius" in her Tudor kitchen or her California abodes.

My father was a mechanic of rage. He fueled himself with anger and swallowed speed. His explosive behavior and mechanized momentum left my brother like roadkill in his path. I doubt he saw himself as a bully, and he resented the thugs who targeted Eddie in the street. Finally, he got his vulnerable son boxing lessons.

To prepare Eddie for self-defense, my parents encouraged him to fight me. I was the oldest but not the biggest. So, there we gathered in the backyard, my brother squaring off, assuming the boxer's stance he learned in a few sessions. He pummeled away. And there I stood, totally unskilled, being pummeled.

My parents' shouts of encouragement to my brother were as rare as the call of an elusive creature, the Elegant Trogon, for an addicted Audubon birdwatcher in Madera Canyon. His gloved fist connected with my face. I froze on the lawn, cupping my nose, bleeding defeat. I went upstairs to splash water on my face and watch the swelling in the bathroom mirror. Neither parent said a word nor ventured upstairs to see how I was.

Years later a specialist affirmed the efficacy of the boxing lessons. I had a deviated septum. He did not think a nose job would alleviate allergies or reduce bouts of sinusitis, so I did not have one. No procedure could fix my nose or my childhood. Some breaks never heal.

I immediately forgave my brother. After all, we were not adversaries. We both suffered chronic nightmares clouded with a father's fists and a mother's insults. Both of us, belittled and besieged, scripted our vengeance in fantasies of finishing off the bullies. My brother befriended prisoners he treated as a psychologist. I befriended my students and built anti-bullying into the leadership curriculum before ideologues diminished and politicized the intent. Propagandists conflated words with acts of violence and free speech with disinformation. Eddie and I knew the difference.

Eddie mastered the multiplication tables and survived his parents. He got a degree and blazed his first independent hiking trail to the Midwest. There he worked with the criminally insane in prisons and hospitals. In twenty years, he did not miss one day of work. He asked a woman to marry him. Another man had just rejected her, and she accepted on the rebound. They had a daughter with a weak heart who underwent several surgeries. Eddie was a compassionate father.

He once told our father he would kill him if he ever raised his hand to his granddaughter again. Our father had done it before, but Tina and I never learned the details from our brother before his death, so it remained a footnote to a father's cruelty. When Eddie died, the wife from whom he had been separated for years told me it might have saved their marriage if she had known what he suffered at his parents' hands. Some secrets are radioactive.

I never saved people from the tidal waves that swamped my dreams. I never saved my sister or brother, leaving the house before they did, leaving them behind. That residual sense of powerlessness is debilitating. You can learn from your parents what not to do. You can save some people from ignorance or despair, hunger or loneliness. And just as you start to exert some control over some areas of your life you run smack into the realization that there are so many things outside your control. It is the AA prayer, to change what you can and accept what you cannot, to live with gratitude and humility and to trust in God.

Our father's final exchanges with Eddie were tumultuous. I hope he was able to know some peace before he closed his eyes, the boy with the lazy eye condition that left him with a patch over the good eye to strengthen the weak one.

I hope Eddie rests in peace. Some breaks never heal, but some do. I say Kaddish for my little brother.

Our home life was bleak.

"Life is a struggle," they told us repeatedly. Words of wisdom from the elders. Words to live by. No wonder the negative seemed more substantial than the positive. I think both parents carried crushed dreams. My father relished his accomplishments as a student at Townsend Harris High School, a competitive public school that took the most academically promising candidates. His degree from City College prepared him for a career as a recording engineer for Columbia Records. His youthful triumphs and party work trumped his family concerns.

If I can believe what he told me, he once worked on Wall Street, but a crash wiped out his shares and he soured on stocks and capitalism. He turned to communism, perhaps to rationalize the failure of his American dream. As a labor organizer at Warner Brothers, he met my mother. He signed on to both struggles, class warfare and the battle between the sexes. He enjoyed individual sports and reviled team sports. He gave us the gift of classical music on records we played repeatedly. But his temper intruded like kettle drums on the peaceful silence of our dreams. He would tolerate no disagreement. He always monopolized the "right" position with percussive intensity.

Perhaps nature and nurture contributed to the dark prism through which I viewed my life. My mother adhered to party doctrine in a cultish fashion that permitted no dissent. When Eddie and I criticized the Soviets for crushing the Prague Spring, she defamed the reactionary college professors she blamed for our apostasy. Most of my professors were socialists, but that was irrelevant.

She found me guilty of "infantile leftism" when I disavowed communist support for the PLO and anti-Israel terrorism. Initially she praised Gorbachev, but when "restructuring" and "openness" disclosed the collapse of a corrupt system, she claimed she would have his Nobel Prize rescinded. No family relationship meant more to her than Marx and Mao. As my husband Len and our family grew in importance, communism diminished. Joy flowed. Despair ebbed. Love restored me to life. It waits there for you beyond dysfunctional family and dystopian rule.

My parents never brought up the essential struggles of life, between good and evil, one's conscience and societal consequences, or legitimate conformity and collective consensus versus individual integrity and the impetus to stand alone. All their struggles referenced totalitarian obedience to party discipline. Their dogma enveloped class struggle. Their personalities engineered parental struggles for control of their children's lives.

As a soon-to-be retired secretary learning to bake bread for the first time, my mother railed against American nationalism. She rallied to "national liberation fronts." Any use of terror to repress "counterrevolutionaries" had her enthusiastic approval. Her appetite for family fights never abated until she was on her death bed in an assisted living facility in La Jolla. She took her certainty to cremation. She had a litmus test and most of us failed. Frances remained impervious to facts, faith, and family ties. She died a Stalinist.

Strangely, many of my family members whose parents were repulsed by her politics now avow a communist narrative. Now they impose a litmus test, and it is my mother's litmus test. They permit me a place in their lives if I self-censor, substitute nostalgia for an ongoing relationship and confine myself to "safe topics." My mother's response to Tiananmen Square reflected the blood-thirsty conclusion that the Chinese communist government should have killed more of the protestors. This suburban woman with an insatiable lust for power found the massacre of ten thousand unarmed dissidents inadequate. What she could not control in her claustrophobic world, she experienced vicariously through communism.

I can imagine the difficult chores and demanding stress of not having enough money. Her apartment did not provide privacy or breathing room. My sleep-deprived mother must have suffered having three children in three-and-a-half years. Eddie's vision and developmental problems appeared at birth. She was overwhelmed, but that provided no excuse for her behavior, or my father's.

No wonder my mother's happiest days occurred in the past when she and her girlfriends became seduced by communism. Enamored by the collective utopian vision they shared, she relished their friendship. They were young. They rode the wave of the future. The professor with whom she had had an affair broke it off. She was stuck. It was indentured servitude she never signed on for with a man she did not love. A bleak reality replaced the bright hopes of her past.

Once married, she did not work outside the home until we were in our teens, but she had none of the labor-saving devices or appliances that might have alleviated some of the stress. Many mothers had no washing machine or dryer, diaper service or disposable diapers. Commercial baby foods were not available. A vacuum cleaner was not affordable.

She always detested housework and delegated chores to us when we were still very young. I can see little Tina standing on a stool to wash dishes at the sink. She dropped a dish when she was spanked. The image is unclear because it is unwelcome.

Before a more affluent age. indulged children with lowered expectations for contributions to running a home, farm, ranch or business, kids did not consider themselves entitled. Before even blue-collar kids were raised to think themselves privileged, kids worked hard. My parents might have been praised for building character, except that the chores were performed under threat of coercion. We heard music on the phonograph, and we heard yelling. They were beasts that music never tamed. "Life is a struggle" permeated every house we lived in but could never call home.

4

TRAUMA

Music played an important part in our lives, from beloved records to tapes and CDs. We incorporated opera subscriptions, radio stations preserving oldies but goodies, jazz riffs, and the occasional live concert into our adult lives. The boys played instruments and sang.

I practice daily on a keyboard, playing simplified classical music and pop hits with little sign of improvement. Despite infinitesimal progress, I manage with dogged determination the demands of a 20-minute daily investment. What might be considered crimes against music help me work my fingers and my brain against the stagnation of age.

There is suffering in life, but there is harmony too. There is work, but it need not be accompanied by demands to take the knee to a totalitarian overseer. Beating does not motivate. Love joins sunshine and rain in irrigating the work ethic. Half-truths of depressed revolutionaries have a long half-life. Do not let them contaminate half or any of yours.

What happened to my nose became a convenient metaphor for my childhood. It hurt at the time. Years passed before I realized how badly I had been damaged. In the final years of my career, terminal exhaustion overwhelmed me. I would hug the walls of the school when someone stopped me to talk because I feared I would pass out. One day I experienced blurry vision and had difficulty maneuvering my feet off the curb. I could not determine the distance. I suffered migraine headaches and started to fall asleep during red lights just blocks from my home.

A doctor performed some neurological tests. He said I suffered from exhaustion and stress. I knew that. He told me I had a broken nose. I did not know that. He sent me to a specialist who told me a deviated septum was common, but he did not think a nose job would alleviate allergies or reduce bouts of sinusitis, so I did not have one. No surgical procedure could fix my nose or my childhood.

When our father reduced us to tears, he chided us for weeping. I banished that word, "weeping," from my vocabulary. He used it to mock us. The word became loathsome, like everything he said or did. We kids spent many hours hiding in the closet to suppress our sobs. Eddie and Tina ventured out on a branch that overhung the garage roof while I remained just inside the window, so we could talk without fear of being overheard. Our parents resented any suggestion of privacy for their kids. It was an obstacle to their control. We wondered if we would live to the age of 21.

When we were grown, Tina and I wondered if Eddie would survive his lymphoma until Memorial Day when we would visit him in the hospital in Ohio. He did not. Tina and I, at Len's urging, found ourselves "hiking" without the third member of our group to a new destination...Wit's End.

Len and I slugged bottled water across the widening waistband of industrial rivers slaking through Pennsylvania Dutch horizons. Sturdy silos and sprawling chemical plants, stretched like limbs of a giant patient hooked up to intensive care. Massive structures resembling IV pulls, tubes, and tanks carried off the poisons. From the van windows we read billboard tabernacles that promised Hershey's chocolate sweet amusement park and family fun.

We drilled through the gaping space between the teeth of Maryland's Cumberland Hills. We watched the spindly branches of diseased trees scratching with splayed fingers at an anemic sky. We passed West Virginia's self-service gas pumps and spotted a triptych of nuclear power plant wasp-waisted cylinders. We skirted shacks in the hollers air brushed by spring's luxuriant green cover. At our destination we rolled to a stop in Huntington with its airport, college, and church steeples.

Across the dawn, Tina flew in from California. Our parents did not attend their son's funeral. For my father, Eddie was an abject failure, and for my mother, an object of pity. "Life is a struggle." We picked Tina up and detoured past the drowned interstate flooded by the Ohio River. No doubt the river dreamed of reclaiming the dimensions of its archetypal inland seas. Watermarks, like bathtub scum, lined houses. The devastation became the souvenir of thirteen inches of run-on rain in two hours. My sister, Len, and I met on folding chairs arranged on the lawn where Eddie's coffin was placed.

Later that day we absorbed cups of hot coffee and heeded the heart's need for warmth. We hugged his widow and his daughter, who had a heart condition as fragile as the flowers left in the waterlogged cemetery. A bulletin board announced the burial of our brother who died at fifty-two years old. The clouds shifted just before a service that broke into ecumenical sunlight. The rays officiated over a final and defiant good-bye. Tina and I searched later that day for shadows, pursuing memories and tracking regret up a path to a small grave just hours old. The grave sits beneath a sheltering tree. Leaves trail in the breeze, part way down a slope overlooking the Ohio River. We say, "Farewell, little brother."

We returned to the Huntington motel and covered each other in salt encrusted embraces. Tina returned to San Francisco. Her lips pressed into a thin line the way the sky meets the sea at the stark moment of sunset when the fiery globe plunges into the depths. Len and I strapped ourselves inside the van and turned away from Ohio, headed for New Jersey and jobs and our sons. We returned to condolence cards and phone calls. I went back to walking the dog and seasonal fruits, spring flowers, a Puccini aria, and all the things our brother would never know again.

My sister and I knew that one member of our trinity had died. Our brother was one part of a brave commando unit that huddled for strategy sessions in the closet and sneaked out onto the roof to nurse battle wounds. We had lost forever the boy who crawled across the bloody borders of childhood with us. He overcame disabilities and channeled rage into achievements. He lived a life of purpose, filled with a new family, dedication to his work, and water skiing.

I wanted to tell my brother that I would carry him in a pocket in my heart. I wanted to tell him that it is not guilt but rather fugitive grief I carry. I could not save him from his childhood or cancer. My offer of a bone marrow transplant was rejected by his doctor. How ironic that my diagnosis as an octogenarian was a blood cancer, Multiple Myeloma. Due to my age, I was not a candidate for the transplant my son offered me. I have enjoyed three decades more than my brother had. During that time, I realized that only God could have saved him.

My parents rejected God in their determination to be gods. My parents were arrogant in their assertions. I was arrogant in my fantasies. We empowered ourselves to be evil or egotistical. We were powerless in our ability to do great things for others. We could not even correct our hubris. The devil exists, not only when he convinces us he does not. He exists when he embeds himself in our ego, convincing us we are gods.

We control very little, which is why power-crazed delusional communists pile up corpses. We would do well to exert self-control. Command and control governments shrink liberty and supersize tyranny. Cancer killed my brother. It afflicts me. Communism is more lethal. I know death is unavoidable, as is the existence of evil.

I confront my own mortality with a probable diagnosis and cause of death printed on it. I relinquish my guilt and grief for things I could not control. Life can bring less suffering when you surrender an arrogant determination to manipulate the lives of others. It offers more than just suffering when you acknowledge the beauty and goodness. The clock and calendar tell me to shatter the bleak prism. I still have time. You do, too.

A woman might wear her beauty the way a newly appointed sheriff pins on a bright, shiny new badge. A public statement. A source of pride. My younger sister was beautiful. She still is. In our family, assets could become liabilities. Anyone out there could see that Tina was exceptionally beautiful. They just never knew the price she paid for her sociability, her style, her intellect, and her talents. She stepped into adolescence as though she had just finished a two-hour roller-skating session, removed her skates, switched into shoes, and taken her first and momentarily unsteady steps. Of course, our mother could try to keep her off balance.

She did not challenge, but neither did she confirm, my sister's gifts. She issued warnings designed to make her uncomfortable in her own skin, such as how to avoid having a boy kiss you. Tina said, "But what if you want him to kiss you?" Undaunted, our mother continued to be judgmental and censorious. She was Machiavellian, simultaneously distant and intrusive.

Typical red diaper babies went to left-wing camps with Russian folk songs accompanied by balalaikas. They flew to youth festivals abroad. We did not get to go anywhere. Many communist parents had liberal, libertine, or bohemian views about sexuality. Our parents were Mr. and Mrs. Cotton Mather. Puritans, maybe Inquisitors, they regarded their children's burgeoning sexuality as a threat. They wanted us to wear hair shirts of self-denial.

Most of our clothes arrived as hand-me-downs in cartons shipped by wealthy and estranged cousins we never got to meet. My sister and I managed to salvage a few bras we secreted away in the bottoms of our bureau drawers. We could never trust our parents with the truth. They never told us the truth about who they were, what they did, or what transpired in the Soviet Union or the Communist Party, USA. They gave us communism and denied us appropriate underwear as the foundation for the great struggles of life.

My mother spotted a bra I wore while we tried on clothes on a particular occasion. She ripped it off me. When I finally got my period, I would hide the sanitary napkins, sneaking them out of the house into the garbage can alongside the garage. She once told me, "The thought of you kissing your boyfriend makes me sick." Another time she said, "The thought of you having your boyfriend's children makes me sick."

I avoided her as much as possible for the duration of my pregnancies. I enjoyed my pregnancies in any other company. They were both boys. What a relief. They would not look like me. I thought how fortunate for them to have a gender's worth of distance at the end of the umbilical cord.

My sister never experienced an awkward stage, an acne-afflicted skin or a stage when she was less than spectacularly unforgettable. She developed normally, advancing from child to mature adolescent with the ease of Hollywood stars like Liz Taylor and Natalie Wood. I was a late bloomer. In a town where my peers started sprouting underarm hair, breasts, and the other accoutrements of sexuality as pre-teens, I entered my fifteenth year on a wing and a prayer.

To be pretty in the fifties meant having legs thick as Corinthian columns and breasts like balconies. My profile was spaghetti thin. One night I completed a school assignment that elicited my father's compliment. "You're quite a woman," he stated in a rare moment of recognition. "Not yet," corrected my mother. I could have killed her.

Neither Tina nor I were content with secondhand clothes, but she did something about it. She got a part time job after school. Her boss was none other than the father of one of my high school friends. I used to enjoy sleep overs at her house where we ate turkey TV dinners at her split-level home. We prepared Social Studies maps with colored pencils on giant pieces of heavy construction paper and watched horror movies. My friend's mother had manicured talons like a raptor's that curved over surfaces. She never noticed, or chose not to, when her husband harassed my sister.

The televised monsters were laughable. Her husband's behavior, cornering Tina on a stepladder taking down stock to try to feel her up, was truly monstrous and not at all laughable. She did not quit immediately. Maybe the need to earn money to have an iota of independence and control and buy plaid pleated skirts and sweaters at other more fashionable stores proved stronger than the need to protect herself from abuse.

Maybe abuse had become an assumption. The store owner, my friend's father, was not too embarrassed to do what he did. Perhaps she was too embarrassed to talk about it. She did not tell me about it until years later. She quit. He and his wife closed the store and moved to a more "desirable" town in search of a "better" class of people.

But the sinister creep did not move out of our lives until he arranged to pick up his daughter and me and my date from a high school dance and drive us to the local pizzeria. He engineered the seating so that his daughter sat on my date's lap. Then he invited my boyfriend to his country club, persuading him that both he and his daughter had more to offer than I did. For Tina and me, encounters with that family exploded illusions we harbored about other people's "normal" families. We might have crazier parents and less money than most of our friends, but we had the strength to survive. We deserved better.

Tina grew taller than I did. She had a voluptuous figure, gorgeous face, and a Renaissance painting halo of long red hair. She was smart. She wrote a good number of her boyfriend's college papers. She was creative and talented. All her friends scrambled to spend time with her. Boys and later, men, lined up to date her. She walked an imaginary runway with a natural grace. Hers was not the affected flamboyance of models whose spin was short-lived and commercially dictated.

She might easily have surrendered like a sleepwalker bereft of dreams. Her talents might have disappeared, like pentimento, or into the negative space in a Japanese print. Her voice could have been lost on the thin expanse of air banished by the batting of a solitary seabird's wings.

She could have spent her time trying to catch her own late-afternoon shadow. Her independent spirit might have succumbed to doubt when the tide washed away footprints before she made them. Not Tina.

She said what she thought. She fed her appetite for independence. Bludgeoned since birth, she endured the belittling and the beatings. She emerged a glorious woman from the depths of hell, a tribute to her and not to nature or nurture.

Our dog Skippy grew fat on the inedible food my mother prepared. She served up her discontent at every meal and I was famished for everything. I weighed only 98 pounds when I left for college. While my classmates criticized the cafeteria, I found in institutionalized cooking a nineteen-pound shield from the childhood I just barely survived.

We slipped scraps of meat cooked to charcoal under the table to our appreciative mutt. The dog served as our confidante. She licked our faces after our parents beat us. We had gotten the dog when we moved to New Jersey. I was 7 or 8. The dog died when I was a freshman in college. We all cried.

Decades later, when our mother died, I did not cry. Tina did. She made a last trip to visit her in the nursing home and told her she loved her. I do not remember clearly, but I hope that our mother told Tina she loved her. Our mother had expressed her own ambivalence about her mate's treatment of their daughter, the torrents of temper, and the constant threat of violence. She did have concerns about Tina's future.

Her beautiful redheaded baby shared the "painting" gene with her. I believe that she did not act decisively to affirm the love she felt for Tina. She offered no protection from physical abuse and levelled her own emotional abuse. In any event, our mother died as she lived, a stranger to normal maternal, unconditional love for her children from the depths of her hollowed-out heart.

For my sister and me, resolution of fractured relationships remains a full-time job. As adults with perspective, we refuse to keep that longed-for resolution on the front burners. We treasure our lives, and wonderful memories to cultivate like gardens of perennials. We have each other. We both have loving husbands. Life has always been so much more than just struggle, and all the sweeter for all that.

Our mother, Frances, never told Tina she loved her. She died as she had lived, a Stalinist. She followed the totalitarian trajectory to the end. Sociopaths deserve to be moved to back burners, if not totally removed from our concerns. Our mother died. Then our father died. We survived and waited longer than we should have to claim our right to be happy.

Now we make up for lost time. Do not lose your way and your time clinging to attic portraits of dark Dorian Grey deceptions. The truth lives in your love. Paint a portrait of faith and family. Paint your own smile.

5

BITTER CANYON

As a child, despair and dialectic marked the latitude and longitude of my position in life. The "life is a struggle" breast milk I was fed surely soured my capacity for joy. Hope should have swum at the confluence of fantasy and fear. Instead, hope acted like a goldfish floating belly up in a glass bowl. On moon-spackled nights, I searched the ceiling for tropical coves along soda pop seas. I dreamed of family reconciliation while awake. Unkempt memories conspired against a neat chronology. Still, I wanted to step outside and feel small bites of moonlight on my fugitive heels. I wanted to throw my head back beneath cello strings of night and swallow whole mouthfuls of stars on my path to victory in life.

Remembering involves watching a fever recede. Degree by degree, illusions retreat behind eyelids. Then with a blink, your temperature registers 98.6 again. Normal. Nostalgia's only keepsake may be the pressed, dried flower of fidelity. But once it is picked, the blossom dies. As mentioned earlier, the past is a kaleidoscope. Its bits and pieces of distinct color, shape, and size twist on the slightest caprice or purposeful turn into new configurations.

Recollections rearrange themselves into a shimmering constellation that moves across the sky. And even if you can chart the heavenly bodies of yesteryear, the light of hope and illusion remains long after the star has burnt out. You cannot know if the universal truth contained in memories of your life expands or contracts. Your recollections might resonate with your readers. Their unique stories might merge with the universal themes that ebb and flow across centuries and continents.

Beneath the scab of childhood sorrow lies Howe Caverns, filled with stalactites of wonderment and triumph and stalagmites of shame and revulsion.

Sharp incisors grow from both jaws, threatening to slam shut on the truth. Who I used to be remains an enigma. What am I to make of it all? It would take a Jurassic Park scientist to work with the DNA of the monsters I have fought and fled to bring them back to life on the pages of this MemNoir. My original title summoned the darkness in my past. In the act of revision, I discovered the excessively narrow and unwarranted emphasis on the negative. The chronicles capture a journey from darkness into light.

The yellow brick road occasionally brightened the landscape of my childhood. Images of the gulag often blighted my path. When I revisit that landscape, I can mourn, a hostage among the headstones. Or I can dress in camouflage, a bandoleer of retribution slung across my chest, and a bulletproof vest to protect my heart. I can go back for vengeance and leave carnage in my wake. I could carry one piece of "carrion luggage," a body bag. I prefer my newer carryon luggage.

My memory houses love and hate entangled in mythic ferocity. It remains to be seen if setting out on the keyboard in search of truth will lead me to adventure at the border of "a wine-dark sea." Odysseus bested monsters to return to his faithful love, Penelope. He journeyed from darkness into light.

Like most happy kids, I could sometimes live in the slam dunk moment. Like most unhappy kids, I could operate my own time machine, reversing into memory, then shift gears into the tire-squealing fast forward of anticipation. Growing up I noticed that my fears and fantasies would turn up inevitably like single socks at the bottom of the family laundry basket.

I do not really remember having had poliomyelitis. I associated my recovery with pulling on heavy cloth stockings before walking to elementary school just blocks from home. It did not stop me from continuing ballet lessons from a

Danish teacher in someone's furnished basement. After classes I walked home on cold nights, brushing snow from hedges. I never gave up the control required to do a cartwheel. But the brush with polio did not prevent me from walking or dancing. Now I reminisce about the unfettered joy of movement while nursing the impact of scoliosis, arthritis, a compressed disc and stenosis on my back. If you live long enough, some painful memories fade while other pains intensify.

Severe insomnia plagued me for much of my life. It is a cruel word. Four syllables share a one-word womb like baby tiger sharks. One eats the others to be born only to continue killing and eating in a wider world. Consider the benefits of insomnia. It beats sleep into retreat, thus staving off nightmares. Insomnia becomes a lover for the besieged, providing time for oneself. It offers time to think and to worry oneself into weariness, and perhaps, dreams. But having insomnia as a kid means succumbing to a seducer of exhaustion before the age of consent. So, lots of the things that made my daylight hours unbearable intruded on the sanctuary of sleep as well.

Insomnia sets fire to the pulse points, leaving you ravaged by the morning sun. You think you could stare straight into a scalding corona and drive it mad. Nightmares, scary daydreams, and insomnia have something in common. They form three spokes radiating from a single hub of fear. Then again, there is something good to be said for insomnia. It proved to be better than being buried alive. I thought I would be buried alive, alone. I would scrape and scratch beneath crumbling dirt in a sealed box to no avail.

Solitude is a mountain of secrets that not even friendship can climb. Loneliness feels like a birthday party with no guests. People would think I died, while I touched the coffin all around, beating on a lid I could not lift. I would find myself trapped in the stomach-churning revelation of my own stupidity. Why did I keep revisiting my fears? Why did I keep so many appointments with mortality when I was still very much alive?

I always thought that on some cosmic scale I would not carry very much weight. I negotiated. When I went fishing, I would always let anything I did not plan to eat off the hook and wish that life had done the same for me. Truth seemed to be my crushed fingers caught in the car door of my own decisions and ill-fated destiny.

During insomniac bouts in high school, I read enough Russian novels to know that our appetites bring death on board. There were galas and nesting dolls. There were handsome nobles and young women swept up by waltz partners, love, and war. Tolstoy and the team of Russian literary spiritual savants depicted drunk peasants in the fields and aristocratic characters in the palaces. I turned page after page until I finally dropped off and an insistent alarm ended a brief slumber.

I could not save my brother or my sister, my cousins or my aunts, my uncle or my grandfather. My fear of death crippled me. I worried about it for so long that after I surprised myself by surviving adolescence, I stopped worrying about it altogether.

You have the time, peace and quiet to concentrate on your fears when you are still awake, long after you have completed the last homework assignment. My eyes refused to shut before I reviewed the last irregular Spanish verb, set the last jumbo roller in my thick hair, and read the concluding chapter of a fat Tolstoy novel. Still awake, I listened to Barry Gray's final sign off on the transistor radio late night talk show. I was still up to track the sound of a train whistling halfway across Bergenfield. Then you have the time, peace and quiet to concentrate on your fears.

Insomnia allows you to bring down the gods. Even pagan rituals to polytheistic gods cannot save them from the defiant rejection of sleep-deniers. A defective dreamcatcher swings from the rearview mirror of memory. It sifts shards of nightmares, catching them in the net and scarring sleep. A properly functioning dreamcatcher would be metronome mobile, swinging to the treble as well as the base. Such a dreamcatcher would syncopate with the sweet sunflower, the smiles that sway the heart, and the spirits that soar on candy apple currents. The insomniac penetrates the deficiency of the dreamcatcher. Insomnia defeats the religious artifacts of fallen gods.

There are parents who insist on stretching possibilities against the thin fabric of night. They disturb the sleep of their children. Their revolutions eat their young. Mortality sits inside each nesting doll within which a smaller doll sits. The Russian dolls, each enclosing a smaller one, stand silent, harboring secrets. Over time decades of oceans enclose smaller bodies, lakes, ponds and puddles. Like the smallest of the Russian dolls, they contain the amniotic fluid in which we swim. They envelop the tears that we shed swimming into birth.

What diminished prospects for joy remain buried by abusive parents in the catacombs of childhood! They lock laughter in a vault. Dust motes swirl above ancient arguments. Forests freeze with blood. Closed doors swing open. Your face is something for your mother to smack while you stand there halfway down the stairs, your girlfriend staring in amazement at the bottom.

A smack across the face punishes you for reading the letter addressed to you. It informs you that you have been denied a scholarship to a prestigious private college. You take a few moments to register the disappointment before handing over the letter. My parents resent an inexcusable delay, a demand for privacy. Whatever brings you to your knees, submission or supplication serves the same aim. Childhood confers no immunity. You have no autonomy. You have no right to your own feelings in the workers' paradise in which you are raised.

You find yourself pressed between the mildewed pages of memory consisting of backhand slaps of insult. You relate to confused desiccated flowers that slip out to bloom in the nightmare distances between cold stars. Years later you sleep soundly in your husband's arms, holding separate dreams entangled in shared lives. The night is the repository of more than the horrific dreams that finally start to fade. It is the nesting place for joy that morning light illuminates.

Returning to childhood, I remember that obscurity enable me to grow up without wearing out my welcome. All paths appear laced with adhesive cobwebs. Language is the filigree of false tongues. Lies are legend, the latitude of misplaced trust and the longitude of raised hands that encircle possibility and return with resignation to back pockets. You might as well shade land masses with nuance and color oceans indifferent.

I learned to circumnavigate expedience and multiple mistakes on the scale of miles. I learned to be invisible. Not being noticed meant avoiding being beaten.

In a world of orphans and unloved children, parents exist as artifacts, relics, and remnants lifted surreptitiously from archaeological digs. Parents, like some pharaohs, carry a curse. Their children cannot wait to bury them along with other old things that stalk their dreams.

I understood later that all children experience exposure to crises. They suffer shame and guilt, and they carry scars of adolescence deeper than acne, because that is part of the human experience. Joys as well as sorrows and hopes as well as fears characterize the typical lives of children cultivated by their loving parents. Abusive homes activate negative attitudes. Recalibration of perceptions opens the path to a more joy-filled reality. How things were need not predict how they will always be. Being born into a dysfunctional family need not become a terrifying destiny.

Not all parents strive to transform human nature into a socially engineered, ideologically superior Soviet worker. Most parents try to raise their children in conformity with Western Judeo-Christian culture. They still make mistakes but are redeemed by the love in which they wrap their families. I discovered later that grown children mourn the passing of parents with grief and gratitude unmitigated by ambivalence. I learned to be happy for them while understanding what I missed.

What I went through was not normal. I started out alone, alienated and abused. I emerged from dysfunctionality and dystopia. I embraced faith, family, and freedom. Fear is not my fate or yours.

For a long time, I had an inventory of fears that encircled my happiest moments, strung out like poppet beads across the neck of my childhood. The worries resided in the double helix of my political birth family and the close-to-home casualties of communism.

I shall tell you about friendly fire and getting thrown out of the house. Some things I tell because I want to remember. And when I do, you will understand why you could have reached me at Bitter Canyon.

For years, I never cried over the passing of an old person. I never mourned the death of illusion. I felt like I would get left behind. I never imagined I would outlive my fears or bury my parents who ended up choosing cremation. I clung to the conclusion that I never had a vacation I did not work too hard for or indulged a laugh uncensored. I never inherited anything beyond loss or assumed a sunrise. I never threw back my head, mare-crazed, against a black sky shredded with stars. I never got a grip on a pebble alongside a licorice river without formulating goodbye and throwing it all away.

    I have never written a poem or ridden a bike going faster and faster down a long hill that winds through a canyon with just the whoosh of wind blowing my thoughts and no helmet to keep anything in order. I never experienced the sheer joy of everything in that popsicle moment of leaping right off the edge of the world without landing in Bitter Canyon and some sort of ending...until recently. Now I empty this worn-out litany of childhood complaints. I replace it with a sun-bright walk around the rim of the canyon and find that I cannot stop smiling.

6

ON MY TOES

As a kid, I figured out that sacrificing what I wanted, and stealing, were two ways to get something for nothing. On the few occasions when our parents offered us a toy, I always refused. "You cannot afford this. You need the money," I would tell them, aware that self-denial got me recognition. My brother might get a dump truck and my sister, a small stuffed animal. Martyrdom meant I never exercised choice, identifying what I wanted, or claiming it. Martyrdom meant momentary approval, which brought me as close to affection as I could get.

Tina and I took dancing lessons. We took ballet, toe, tap and acrobatics. She remained a good dancer and still moves around the dance floors of California and Hawaiian clubs with her partner and husband. Back then, we dressed for recitals in cancan costumes of strawberry and turquoise satin. Our mother demonstrated capability with her Singer sewing machine and patterns. She made us a number of outfits. Tina, too, learned to sew and turned out some attractive clothes. I never learned to sew. I received an "incomplete" in eighth grade home economics for failing to finish an apron. As a parent, I could replace a button and darn a sock, but that was it.

Just before the opening number of one dance recital on a school stage, my girlfriend noticed that she did not have her tiara. I immediately handed her mine after she burst into tears. She was my friend, and she was crying. I did not care that much about the tiara. At the end of the program, members of the audience congratulated me, the one dancer on a stage crammed with little girls who stood out for her bare head. I had shown up like a waxy green pepper on a baker's dozen glazed white doughnuts. I stood out on my toes, an unexpected outcome. I was happy.

What I could not claim publicly, I could swipe. I remember feeling very small. A clerk in a store in Boston had just caught me stealing. I rarely had any money, and I was always hungry like a character in a Dickens novel. Perhaps I should set the stage for the theft. My father always insisted on sitting at the head of the table, even though we had a round table. A summons to a meal signaled an invitation to a battleground.

My mother would provoke him to spontaneous combustion with a word. Meals were summonses to entrapment and explosions of anger and violence. A stick of purloined chewing gum tasted better than a home-cooked meal. I remember feeling very small at the family dining table as well as at the scene of my crime. Trouble pursued me everywhere.

Mealtimes were not conducive to eating. The three of us would sit silently, eyes wide with apprehension. We waited to see which one of us our parents would address next. First the yelling. Then, the beating. Chairs were shoved back from the table. Footsteps pounded on the stairs. A bedroom door would be slammed open and then slammed shut.

Victor followed us upstairs to administer our punishment while our mother continued to scream from below. The only time she did not encourage him occurred when he slapped her hard against the side of the head in the kitchen. So, it seemed quite strangely unimaginable that I committed my act of theft while visiting generous and beloved relatives in Boston, not in my parents' home.

That poses one of the problems with recollection. Everything sits in a junk drawer, but you do not know the precise location. Searching through the junk drawer, you cannot find one memory without picking up lots of other stuff.

At Aunt Gail's house, she, my Uncle Carl, or one of my cousins gave me a nickel. I walked a couple of blocks down a hill to a store and stood in front of the gum display next to the register. I must have stood there for a suspiciously long time debating the relative merits of Clark's Teaberry and Blackjack, a licorice-flavored gum. They were my favorites. My aunt kept her house well provisioned with foods both delicious and delectable. I chose the pack of gum as a pure luxury. I tried to take two for the price of one. I stole.

I can see myself taking the gum off the rack and concealing it. I can see myself paying for the other. Then the man looms over me. He has dark, dark hair, and his eyes are dark with anger. "I could send you to jail," he tells me. I have no reason to disbelieve him. I relinquish the stolen gum and complete my purchase. The man ushers me out the door.

The whole way back I feel like a rabbit that has blundered into a convention of hounds. I know vulnerability. I know criminality. I know shame and guilt.

When I first harvested the shame that still shadows me, I was in my fifties, sometime in the afternoon of my life. Years after the crime, I reflected that I disappointed my parents unless I relinquished something I wanted. I disappointed my myself when I took something I wanted. Even when I did not have to hear my parents calling me names, I could not stop calling myself names. My achievements might be considerable, but the pluses always felt ephemeral, transitory, and insubstantial. My shortcomings, vices, and transgressions were the footprints cast in stone at my Hollywood Walk of Infamy.

I could calibrate the pluses and minuses of my life. The gravity-weighted minus end of the seesaw positioned itself firmly on the ground. The plus end, unburdened by self-esteem, always catapulted an inadequate me into the air. My parents may have disinherited me, but my personally infamous legacy looms large. I still feel small.

If I lived and wrote as a Beat poet, I could have done a "list" poem about times I felt small. I am six years old and very, very small. I am looking up at an elevator door that will not open. Walls surround me. I might have been going up to my family's Washington Heights apartment, or down to the street for unsupervised, unstructured play in relative safety. Maybe I held a piece of chalk or a pink and very bouncy Spaulding rubber ball in one hand. Trapped, I could not find anything reassuring to hold on to. Here I found myself alone, trapped, wanting to get out. Confined. Claustrophobic.

As a graduate student at Columbia, I must take an elevator in the subway. As a caseworker in central and East Harlem, I ride trains to visit clients atop six story walkups. The train tunnels are dark, and the cars are packed. Fans sometimes fail and lights dim. Trains stall and I sit or hold a strap handle between equally impatient riders. Sweat springs from my palms and forehead. Hysteria mounts, and the air seems to disappear. I know I am claustrophobic. I do not know why until my father mentions that an old friend of his does not take the subway because of his claustrophobia.

When I reveal my problem, Victor laughs. He tells me that when I was six, I was trapped in an elevator for half an hour. I had forgotten that until I had to cram into the packed elevator to reach Columbia. The truth does not set me free. During my thirty-year career as an educator, I avoided school elevators. I learned more, dispensed more guidance, and deterred more fights by climbing flights of stairs. I motivated more students and avoided more anxiety by walking many steps than I would have by taking the elevator.

For meetings in Brooklyn at the Board of Education, I climb eight flights of stairs to meetings. At the doctor's office I take three floors on foot rather than ride an elevator. At a resort with family members alongside, sometimes alone, I will take an elevator, but I always breathe a sigh of relief when the doors open and I can bolt out. Besides, fear, like extra pounds, tends to hang on. Phobias, like extra weight, keep you from aging well. The fear and phobias have finally abated.

If I cannot keep my own secrets, why would I expect anyone else to? You know now that I can sacrifice or steal what I want. I will let you play with my doll with a dozen different designer outfits. After all, I have already changed her clothes many times and rearranged her hairdo less skillfully. If you desire to play with the truth, you might discover it has been rearranged. Secrets culled from the past do not always tell the truth. Like the used and discarded doll, my recollected truth is now slightly less recognizable than when it was new. What is less desirable than a memory of shameful secrets?

One day when I was five or six, I was playing across the street with my girlfriend. A car pulled up and a man called through the window, "Get in the car little girls, and I'll give you candy." My friend walked towards the door. I grabbed her back yelling, "No, no, my mommy said 'no.'" And one day I found myself stuck in an elevator for thirty minutes. So, I owe my life to my mother's words while my father's words came too late to make any difference at all.

I want to write my own ending. A seagull flies over the New Jersey Turnpike, amid the tang of ocean and jet fumes overhead. I have a deceased mother. How little my mother had to teach me about how to reach my sons. How strange I thought it was that I settled in the suburbs. I never figured out how to communicate lingering questions or agnostic interests from the depths of my secret, marred soul.

Poem after poem, I write about and my sons. One umbilical cord removed from each generation, I look across at the city in which part of me always wanted to live. I loved walking the streets and exploring neighborhoods. I appreciated the anonymity of crowds and the chance to shine at a poetry reading or in a classroom. I devoured the unpredictability of each moment and the prospect of losing and finding myself anew. I did not know whether it was the better part of me that ended up on the wrong side of the Hudson River.

I realized that the better part of me crossed into my husband's life and raised our sons in the suburbs. We found the better part of life crossing the Mississippi from East Coast careers to Arizona retirement. The better part of old age precipitated our crossing back after fifteen fabulous years to reunite with our sons and grandchildren on the East Coast.

7

SOVIET INSANITY

My parents carried on a long-distance love affair with the Soviet Union their entire adult lives. They clung to ideology like lice to hair follicles. Despite their allegiance to the party, they claimed they were expelled in an internecine struggle. I later learned that some members quit to hide their membership. Regardless of the real explanation, signing over the skepticism they reserved for America never got them very far in party circles.

But my father persisted in dreaming of concentric circles of distance from the sinking pebble of our family destiny. While we still lived under his roof, he was offered a promotion, an assignment of several years' duration with his recording company abroad.

One morning there was talk of Italy that promised to alter the family dynamics. Perusing the Sunday Times travel section, our eyes focused like red darts on a military map encircling Italy. Funnels of adventure rose from my father's pipe along with the whisps of the possibility of a job transfer out of the blue-collar, conservative, Catholic Bergenfield he hated. My brother would live thousands of miles from the neighbors who controlled their territory the way the Mafia controlled Sicily. My mother sifted plans like flour, working her strategic piecrust dough.

For three months, my father commandeered our collective dreams. He commanded the couch and towered in the living room like Vesuvius, counting down the days until we moved to Florence. Wearing a European beret and riding a bicycle, he reconnoitered the local library for archaeology books. All his life had been a dry run for this three-year transfer to adventure in Italy.

One night, the lava of wounded dreams lit the end of his cigar. The lines of his mouth set like the friezes on the walls of Pompeii. He snarled the disappointment of a hungry lion prowling the Coliseum. That night, we watched television as the Arno River delivered a Florentine flood. It carried off cats, priceless antiquities and works of art. That night I understood that Italy was off. And my brother said, "who wants to learn Italian anyhow?"

For years, my mother had to content herself with trips to planned events in New York State parks. With Italy off the agenda, she scheduled excursions to domestic bastions of communism. Left-wing newspapers and magazines lay strewn across the picnic tables laden with sandwich wrappers and crusts, soggy potato chips and slivers of pickle. The castanets of cicadas and the loose gravel pitch of Pete Seeger serenaded us. Leftists of all types scattered on blankets spread on the grass. My mother, content in her element, hoped to make it mine.

My parents scheduled trips to conferences and lectures in NYC featuring socialist realism. The unapologetic husband of playwright Lorraine Hansberry clung to the artistic restraints imposed by subservience to communism. Posters and books about US racism featured Paul Robeson as the heroic American battling the original sins of US capitalism, enslavement, exploitation, and segregation of blacks. Statistics of racist hangings dominated. Statistics of Soviet mass murders disappeared into a pit of lies.

One panel discussion featured a young Julian Bond. His leftist ties remained unknown. Julian climbed to power and celebrity before cocaine addiction, NAACP radicalization, and the successful infiltration of the civil rights movement by the communist movement came to light. I knew about his ideology. I did not know that it was wrong. I thought he was heroic.

We had lived in a small apartment in upper Manhattan before moving to small houses in blue-collar towns in New Jersey. We had eventually grown up and left home or been thrown out of the last outpost of the Family Gulag. Our parents moved to coastal southern California. From that bastion of bourgeois comfort, they proceeded to conduct costly pilgrimages to the Potemkin Villages of the Soviet Union. They felt they were finally at home for the first time in their lives during the Soviet government-sponsored propaganda tours.

The most important trips Eddie, Tina, and I made were the ones that led us away from home. Still, I went back often to see how the houses aged. I wanted to knock at the front door and go in to climb the stairs to the bedroom I shared with Tina. We would summon Eddie from across the hall and open the closet door. I fully expected to find us all there clustered in the dark, so many rusty stars scraping against the night. When I swiftly retrace my steps, I try to escape that moribund hellhole.

I finally figured out that every reminiscence need not be a beachhead for brutality. I could redecorate the past, one page with description as richly detailed as a Persian carpet, and the next with the spare sketch of a heron posed on a silk screen. On every visit to an old house, I wanted to push wildly into the fray pummeling the past. I knew that one misstep would make me a howling wolf in a steel trap.

Could I open the closet and find my brother and sister and relive those years? I am relieved that I cannot. I could not rewrite that beginning or ending. I am trying now to write a new beginning.

Autumn is a fitting time to write about my mother. September fancies itself part of a season of farewells to departing leaves and dimming, slowly disappearing light. There is the chill of loss and the imperative of atonement. This is the effort I make to leave the past behind.

As an adult and a mother, I live in these moments between madness and music. I light the memorial candle for the unclaimed decades.

Mozart dragged my shadow up the turnpike after I drove my older son back to Rutgers. Our child lived too close to me and my husband to think we were possessed of inordinate wisdom. Len and I find that most of what we had to pass down got stolen while we were out of the house one evening. Intruders robbed

Len's grandfather's pocket watch and my Aunt Gail's gifts to me of her antique bracelet and brooch. No insurance could cover the deductible between birth and memory.

My life seemed to slip from my shoulders like a loosened garment. Much seemed insubstantial. And yet the smell of chocolate macaroons pulled at my nostrils like a farmer's tug on a yoked ox. I enjoyed the mashed hard-boiled egg yolk, crumbs of broken matzoh, slices of nuts and apple drenched in wine and honey, and the spoonful of chopped chicken liver. All this bounty flowered over a forest floor of porcelain for all these years after World War II. Once, starving arms outstretched in dreams reached through barbed wire and smoke for a taste of life, the hope of next year in Jerusalem or anywhere.

Who served us the sorrow that is the uninvited companion to simple pleasures? I removed my glasses and put down the book about a Chinese woman in America. Her story encompassed the anecdotes of distant mountains, the obligatory mists, and someone's starving children. They might have been hers. They were not mine, but they were closer to my own childhood experiences for which nobody organized a feast. Regrettably, it seemed I had gained nothing with which I could console myself for all that I never tasted.

I found that after forty-seven years, I had a book of poems I dared not write, not until my parents' death freed me. Then I could go back to that land where everything would seem smaller now. Even so, I could try to reclaim, like a tragic woman with a pawnbroker's yellowing ticket, the memory of my youth. I could pawn my feelings without having to fear that my parents would tell me, once again, that I got it all wrong. It should be enough for them to know that I realized that. I got so much about my adult life wrong. For a while, I thought it probably too late to do anything much more than climb over the typewriter keys to some far-off mountain and wait for the decades to pass and the mists to clear.

A new day arrived, and the mists eventually cleared. Fortunately, I no longer attribute any acuity to my parents' observations. Their assessments of us and of the world proved invalid.

Holidays are no longer haunted by my legacy of inadequacy. They are times of celebration and joy, family and faith. I am not a communist. I have not fallen for that cult for years. I am a patriotic American and a proud Jew.

More recently, Len took me to Israel to fulfill the Biblical prayer, "Next year in Jerusalem." We flew from the Sonoran Desert of Arizona to the Negev Desert of Israel. I have never visited the Soviet Union. I visited Israel, my spiritual homeland, on the trip of a lifetime.

Decades marked the last time my sister and I saw our mother together. She handed my sister a voodoo doll. She told us we could make a lot of money selling handmade sock voodoo dolls with greeting cards that instructed the purchaser on how to inflict various ailments from the menu on their enemies. She told my sister, a talented painter, to find an artist to design the card. She told me, a poet, to find a writer to script the cards.

When we left the nursing home, my sister handed off the spooky little doll to me. Neither of us wanted this last gift from our mother's hands. My husband took it and flung it out of the window of the car. He had never littered before and never did it again.

We were rid of the horrifying doll. Tina and I still had to dispose of our mother's belittling advice that had a toxic half-life of thousands of years. Her haunting dismissal of our talents withered our souls, for a time. But the curses ended with the help of our husbands and the insights of intervening years. The doll was gone, our mother died, and we were free.

8

HARD TO FOLLOW

I lived in a communist nightmare in the middle of a free country. Growing up in a communist household gave me a head start to a dead end. Here's what my brother and sister and I had that other kids did not. We went on trips to NYC hotels that hosted conferences displaying graphic photos of lynched blacks. We viewed a gallery of photos of Paul Robeson costumed in theatrical garb. We heard tributes to the Abraham Lincoln Brigade. We listened to panel discussions on the primacy of Socialist Realism. Anything an author wrote should promote party policies.

Dissenters deviated from "the truth." The Party exacted a rigid discipline. Party orthodoxy implanted a strong sense of "social justice" in the USSR. It ingrained a sense of social injustice in the USA. As the oldest, I was exposed to more of these expeditions into dystopian deception. More was invested in me. More was expected of me in terms of continuing my parents' family tradition of hatred for the United States, verging on treason of thought that might evolve into action. All I had to do was surrender the skepticism born of free will.

Our athletically inclined father gave the three of us lessons in our New Jersey backyards in archery, fencing, and pogo stick jumping down the driveway. We received nothing conventional. The mere mention of what everyone else did brought beads of sweat to a boil, bubbling like porridge on our parents' foreheads.

Our father did not coach us for team sports.

We attended firework displays at a local public school on Independence Day, but we never attended patriotic parades. Instead, we marched on May Day and Labor Day Parades. I do remember one Easter Parade while we still lived in New York City. I had a straw hat with a ribbon, white gloves, and black Maryjane shoes. My communist parents converted the religious content into something far afield from Easter's meaning. They marched in an Easter parade as pagan to them as the traditional Christmas tree they embraced.

The only institution my parents hated more than the military was the Roman Catholic Church. They labeled neighbors "Churchniks." These neighbors mowed their lawns with conviction, saluted their flag with combat service and affection, and attended church services with regularity. To my parents, the bent head and bent knee symbolized the working man's oppression.

Victor and Frances believed that submission, subservience, and supplication worked hand in hand to oppress the proletariat on behalf of the capitalists. They endorsed the Soviet Constitution that promised rights never delivered. They rejected the foundational documents that acknowledged inalienable rights stemming from God. They held that all "rights" stemmed from the party. The party had the power to enact class equality. Equality of poverty emerged as the only equality delivered by the elites. My parents hated the American view of the constitutional and religious equality of souls and equality before the law.

Once, on a tour showing us the first house we ever owned, the real estate agent announced proudly that the local priest had blessed the walls. I asked how much the house cost without the blessings. Then, I was still my parents' daughter. When I spoke, my child's tongue had teeth.

I learned to hate long before prescriptions replaced resumes in my life. My parents clung to communism from my childhood to the final spins of the season in the death throes of the 20th century. They gave me hand-me-down hatreds as well as clothes. It strikes me as funny how much my parents despised religion and religious people, given the ferocity of their faith in communist orthodoxy. Communist dogma fueled fanaticism. Even liberation theology failed to elicit their praise. All religion was anathema, except communism. Conscience did not exist in their cult.

To prove the existence of God, St. Thomas insisted on an act of bedrock faith from which stemmed all other religious beliefs, buttressed by ritual. My parents' proof of the scientific determinism underpinning Marxism also rested on a foundation of faith. Their twisted mix of analysis and adrenaline constituted their apologia for a cult of criminality, corruption, and carnage. They subscribed to a dialectic that created one totalitarian dystopia after another. They put their faith in communism despite the ideology leading to the deaths of millions upon millions.

My parents hated money. Mostly they hated people who had money. They hated the people who did not have money but who refused to become revolutionaries. They hated revolutionaries who were not Marxists. They hated Marxists who were not Stalinists. They hated traitors and "infantile leftists." They hated Trotskyites. They claimed to love humanity in the abstract. They just so happened to hate the next-door neighbor who attended church services that they detested.

Victor and Frances applied their litmus test of obedience to Marxist orthodoxy to family and friends alike. Kindred souls to Dostoyevsky's Grand Inquisitor, they equated heresy with treason.

In *The Brothers Karamazov*, the Grand Inquisitor does not welcome Jesus Christ. In taking away Christ's freedom, he believes he is sparing Christians the burden of free will. He takes it upon himself to make decisions and exercise control rather than let them wrestle with their conscience and reason. In that warped scenario, Jesus is not only unnecessary but also unwelcome.

My parents were descendants of the Grand Inquisitor. They despised Torquemada but emulated his arrogant intolerance. They crushed their children's spirits to save their secular souls.

In the beginning, there was Marx. And in the end, there was the end of the Soviet Union. Long before that, I fell from political grace. My challenge expelled me from the Garden. They carried out a threat before my senior year of college.

They threw me out of the house in a communist excommunication.

Once they had indoctrinated me to carry on their communist legacy. Later, they denounced me as an apostate.

When I read Dostoyevsky, I discovered another purpose for, and interpretation of, suffering. Dostoyevsky explained the purpose of suffering in *Crime and Punishment*. He traced the path of Raskolnikov from a man who thought himself a god to one who knew better. Determined to break laws and commandments, Raskolnikov murdered an innocent woman. Later, he accepted years of punishment to atone for his sin of hubris. Through suffering he accepted the love of a woman and of God. He welcomed his suffering to save his soul.

How different from the suffering my parents inflicted on their children. They loved the "suffering masses" of humanity in the abstract but hated individuals in the flesh. That included their own flesh and blood. For decades their children heard the echo of their revolutionary perspective: "Life is a struggle." They always meant the class struggle.

We wrestled to interpret that in a new light we could live with. It is a fight against arrogance. Communists are guilty of the intellectual tyranny of absolute certainty. They are willing to use coercion to consolidate power. In the false belief that they can supplant God, authoritarians attempt to remake human nature. We three suffered to free ourselves of propaganda that lodged like a parasite in our systems.

History recounts the fights individuals and civilizations wage against formidable challenges. Apocalyptic threats like disease, hunger, poverty, and war crush cultures and customs. But life remains so much more than the bleak outlook that diminished our childhood. History illuminates the triumphs of transcendence. Individuals elevated by character, courage, and curiosity make significant contributions to the culture.

The exceptionality of Western Civilization and the beauty of our constitutional republic are based on belief in God rather than a belief in communism. Changes wrought by capitalism lifted the standard of living and life span of millions. The average American lives more comfortably, longer, and more securely than kings did a little over a century ago.

Growing up in my parents' house meant a dialectic in the daily commerce of words.

I might have wanted to sing the alphabet, open the window, and swallow the sun. I might have unleashed my ghosts and fantasies in poems. But I knew I could show no stuttering indecision when about taking the "right" position on any and every issue. I had no autonomy.

In one recurring nightmare, I find myself at the zoo. Suddenly, all the cages are unlocked and the big cats escape. I clamber into a cage and try to bar the door with me inside. Blood splashes through the flayed apple peel of my fingers folded around the bars. The tigers and lions prowl outside the cage, stinking of piss and peanuts with their eyes of golden magnets. I cannot tame the cats, and I wake each time as they enter the cage.

I cannot stop the Russian tanks that pounce into Czechoslovakia. My parents stand on a different side of the cage from me. They scream, "What are they teaching you in that reactionary college?!" When I look at photographs of my parents, I know I am not looking at socialism with a human face. There is no Prague Spring. There is only the desolation of Siberian winter. The bullet in the back of the head ends all debates in Lubyanka Prison. Apex predators head the Communist Party. Their hunger cannot be sated.

My parents chose not to sit on comfortable cushions of tradition. They refused to corset themselves in courtesy. In some ways their defiance seemed commendable, but their defiance had striking flaws. They sent mixed messages. They refused to let their children choose the ways in which they would be different. We could not have high school jackets or wear ballerina slippers to school. Those were small things. We also could not select our own principles, values, or beliefs. I could not choose my boyfriend or husband.

Our parents isolated themselves by choice. They wanted us to be isolated. And to a degree, we were. We had to hide the truth about our communist abode. I did not rest my head on pillows of happily ever after. I slept and woke under a waterlogged moon. I lived a guarded life.

I had to duck beneath my desk in fifth grade during civil defense drills. By junior high, I refused to read from the Bible or recite the Lord's Prayer. My parents permitted me to be Jewish only to stay out of school on the High Holy Days in high school. They acquiesced to our Jewishness to mark me as someone different. There was no connection with practicing Jews, people my parents scorned for their fidelity to the Old Testament.

My entry in the daughters of the American Revolution essay contest paid tribute to Marion Anderson. My folks selected a topic dear to communists. They carefully edited my essay. By the time I delivered it, I was unclear as to the authorship. I did not win. I did not deserve to.

9

SEEING THROUGH THE LIES

At home, my sister and I danced in the living room to Stravinsky's "Fire Bird Suite" and Prokofiev's "Romeo and Juliet". We also danced to Dion and the Belmonts and the Everly Brothers. Part of the political rift included my immersion in Dylan's songs and the Saturday sweet spin of Symphony Sid's jazz records. I could see my parents' spines snap to attention at the playing of the Soviet anthem, the International. But we never heard "Hatikvah." It was not until televised showings of James Cagney's stellar performance in "Yankee Doodle Dandy" that Tina and I discovered the patriotic cadence of American pride. One person's musical riff is another person's political rift.

I only read Elie Wiesel's *Souls on Fire* years after having read Eldridge Cleaver's *Soul on Ice*. I played the role of a congenitally conscientious supporter of civil rights. I felt an affinity for all things black. My upbringing led me to feel contempt for all things Jewish.

But time acts like a splinter I must remove from the raw fingertip of memory. Looking back on the rigidity of my family faith, I can diagnose the crippling osteoporosis of the soul with which I was afflicted. Ideology inflamed us, suppressing our immunity to lies.

Our parents are our first teachers. From mine I learned to deplore individualism and deify collectivism. I attacked every subject with the hammer and sickle of transcendent certitude. I attacked people, rhetorically, never physically. And that aggressive stance struck me as okay at first.

Ultimately, cracks like the first fine lines on the frozen surface of a lake begin to appear. Skepticism spreads, a finely traced web. My parents warn against my spring thaw of skepticism. They voice aloud their realization that having had me had been a bad decision. I become a living memorial to their mistake. In betraying communism, I betray them.

Indulge me in the long sweep of your stride. Walk about halfway down the dead-end street to the little white house just at the point where it starts to go down the hill. Two men walk up the steps, rolling like tanks down the front porch to the door. My mother responds to their knock. She listens and then closes the door in their faces. They are FBI agents, she tells me later.

She reminisces about tenant strikes in Harlem and the Peekskill riot. She regales me with tales of a friend who fought in the Abraham Lincoln Brigade in Spain. She recounts how she got rejected to go as a nurse when she passed out at the sight of blood. She elaborates on organizing Warner Brothers, which is how and where she and my father met.

I could not say they fell in love at Warner Brothers. My mother had previously been divorced. She also had an affair with a professor who decided he would give her his love but not his life. Eventually, he broke it off in favor of his wife. My father had previously had a Russian girlfriend.

My parents said their "I dos" to the party. I doubt they fell in love with each other, but they did keep nude photos of my mother in a drawer. One day my brother acted in a fit of pre-adolescent angst, breaking the recording the three of us had made of "Why Do Fools Fall in Love." Our father engineered the session when we visited his recording studio at Columbia Records. Eddie also ripped up the photos. He carried the burden of parental intrusions into his sanity to his deathbed. Parental malignancy metastasized.

My mother spoke of files, phone taps, and being followed. Once we drove to suburban Virginia to visit an older couple, friends of my parents. The guy was an engineer and a communist. My mother said there were FBI agents outside their friends' door every day.

My parents expected all three of us to follow in their footsteps. I could not determine to what extent paranoia possessed my parents. They were absolutely certain of their absolutes. My mother claimed a crowning achievement of her life that she orchestrated Mikhail Gorbachev receiving the Nobel Peace Prize. She regarded as her greatest frustration her inability to deprive him of that prize. Once the twin reforms of glasnost and perestroika touched off the third rail that electrocuted communism, the USSR fell.

She renounced Gorbachev but never communism. I did not know how much of her allegiance to her high ideals turned out to be authentic versus expedient. She rallied to human rights and championed civil liberties only when the United States committed the abuses, real or imagined. When it came to the Soviet Union, my mother relegated civil rights and civil liberties to bourgeois relics of the superstructure. What was a radical cause here was a reactionary cause there. Gradually I rescinded my loyalty to doctrine. A healthy reflux made Marxism harder to swallow. Communism became increasingly difficult for me to follow.

According to the Freedom of Information file, no paper trail exists for my parents. Frances died without ever revealing the extent of their involvement. Victor maintained his distance from my inquiries, which became less frequent as his body odor grew more noxious. Neither ever accepted me in any way. They died as the communists they were to the very end. Neither parent forgave me for making my escape from their ideological stranglehold on my wish upon a star.

I always had a hunger for books. My library card became my ticket to the wet woods and swishing cat's tails of Kipling's *Just So Stories*. That card substituted for my passport to the icy Norse battlefields where "The Twilight of the Gods" was re-enacted every time I read the final chapter. I loved books about archaeology and the excavation of layers upon layers of truth. I loved tracing city grids in ancient Greek labyrinths and Rome's seven hills. I read the war strategies of Winston Churchill. My parents read me to sleep with selections from *The Communist Manifesto* and later regaled me with insights from *The Little Red Book*. They took a photo of me as a toddler in a knit sweater and bonnet "reading" the *Daily*

Worker.

I remain a voracious reader. Now in my eighties, I find myself writing two books, hoping to find readers of my own.

Communist tracts trumped the *New York Times*. I read all my parents gave me, memorizing everything and learning nothing. They equipped me with the survival skills necessary to make my way through the wilderness of the written word when the trail pointed in a particular direction. When the words led me into Orwellian doublespeak, I got lost. I failed to determine my own location, direction, or destination. For too many years I listened to them when my parents told me to follow in their footsteps. The pied pipers of propaganda led me astray. It took Len to eradicate the poisonous roots of my upbringing.

My parents uttered many unforgettable words. When the Chinese government ordered its troops to fire on its citizens who bravely stood up to tanks in Tienanmen Square, my mother complained, "They didn't kill enough of them." When Joan Baez criticized the Pol Pot regime for its genocide, she removed the singer from her slate of progressive icons as swiftly as you might swing a baseball bat. My father, arrogant in his political beliefs, had disdain for any spiritual or religious tradition. He taught us to doubly despise veterans who believed in God and service.

He boasted about a letter received from the Soviet Union acknowledging his offer to join their armed forces to fight the fascists in World War II. Not a sentimental man, he kept that treasured letter of thanks. Having been turned down by the reds, however, he expressed contempt for his American counterparts who volunteered to fight for the United States in the war against fascism. He must have been horrified when his grandson, my older son, Seth, joined the Army.

I had received my marching orders for mandatory attendance at communist events. I attended the obligatory panels, and I attended May Day and Labor Day parades that marked the communist calendar. I sat in rapt attention at conventions focused on Jim Crow. I religiously attended picnics, rallies, and marches. We were carefully taught the songs of *South Pacific*, like "You've Got to be Carefully Taught."

Human rights had validity when the United States got accused of abusing them. Human rights were reactionary relics when applied to the actions of any totalitarian regime operating from the left. It was an *Alice in Wonderland* world, complete with the queen yelling, "Off with their heads." One day, one of those heads would be mine.

Our parents would not allow us to conform to peer culture. They pressured us to conform to the communist catechism. We had no autonomy. We could not choose the country to which we felt allegiance. We could not decide when to be different. Questioning their beliefs displayed heresy, and I was anathema.

Sometimes my siblings and I got into trouble for taking an idea too seriously. I took my sister to the March on Washington in 1963. I was in college, and she was in high school. I took a day off from work that tumultuous summer. I purchased two round trip-chartered bus tickets for us and off we went. Our parents might have been frightened about the prospect of violence, but they had had no qualms about shepherding us to other marches or rallies.

They did not worry about something awful happening to us. They worried about us taking control of our own lives. As it happened, something was happening to us. Our initiative threatened their authority and endangered their control. Even a shared belief in civil rights meant nothing when we acted without their permission.

A few years later, I met my mother, each of us on either side of a New York City policeman on horseback. His bully club waved wildly at an unruly demonstration against George Wallace's speech at Madison Square Garden. After the March on Washington, my parents never asked us about our experience or our reflections on that historic mobilization. They never credited us with a modicum of courage or cared about what we had learned. We had disobeyed. That was enough. No attendance at later politically correct events assuaged the disobedience.

Dr. King's admonition to judge each person by the content of his character rather than the color of his skin emerged as one lesson we took from our childhood. It germinated into a lifelong principle. Our parents had no interest in watching that flower bloom.

My parents were Stalinists in terms of their parenting philosophy and practices. Thus, the personal and political for me were the intricately intertwined strands of the double helix. My parents inflicted punishment for thoughts and deeds. They believed in power. They believed in torturing and killing their opponents. Terror ruled our home life. The vanguard was invincible.

As parents of two, we made the mistake of visiting them at their apartment just before returning from our family vacation in California. My younger son, Jake, noticed my mother's strange behavior. "She just kept saying 'uh huh' to get you to be quiet, but not to listen or agree. She looked like a witch." It was a moment of clarity for me. My sons selected their favorite bedtime books. Like all kids they enjoyed legends and myths, and their *Just So Stories*. Still, right up until Jake's observations, I thought both boys had relied upon books for their concept of witches.

I assigned my sons summer reading lists. They practiced their instruments and read after a full day at camp. They learned within limits about suffering and injustice, war and poverty. The Four Horsemen of the Apocalypse never invaded their dreams. They learned to distinguish heroes from villains and virtues from vices. They had their share of temper tantrums and teen withdrawals into silence. They teased each other and learned to love each other deeply. They nibbled slivers of truth we served. They rejected some of our ideas and restrictions. But mostly they knew we loved them without reserve, judgment, or condition.

We continue to be close to this day, having moved back east for proximity. We spend time with each other to enrich our lives with the experience of family.

We did not always exercise sufficient patience with them or with each other. We offered them some aspects of ourselves they might have judged "positive role models." We taught them what to be and what not to be, sometimes by example.

But we never descended into the witches and monsters inhabiting their worlds the way my parents inhabited mine and my siblings' worlds. My younger son called out my mother's poisonous center. He identified the monster who dwelt at her core. Emergence meant the recognition of evil, and transcendence meant turning away from evil. I did my best to incorporate that lesson.

10

CRYING FOR THEM AND ME

I was born in September to a woman who would have trouble celebrating my birth in the years to come. Her post-partum depression extended into my adulthood. I picture her as a grazing animal, alone, on a golden slope covered in sweet grass surrounded by wildflowers. By day she chews over her hatreds. By night she eats herself alive with regret.

Once she sent me a card around the holidays. It was not for Christmas, which she celebrated but in which she did not believe. It was not for Hanukkah, which she believed in not celebrating. It was a secular, seasonal card with an all-purpose greeting. My mother signed it simply, "Frances."

I was born in Manhattan. Across the wet expanse of tall grass in the Meadowlands, the city shines. It appears all glass and glitter. All night neon staccato plays. It beats in counterpoint to sax solos echoing off concrete canyons. I live in the suburbs, but I work and dream in the city. I wonder what would have happened to me had I lived where stars stitch the broken jaw of the Manhattan skyline.

Sharing anecdotes in bars, strangers swallow lite beer. They toe tap to a solitary tune no one else can hear. They stage community. They pretend that in their too small apartments they left not only a cat but the first act of a play. Maybe lodging in the faded upholstered sofa, they left something else creative. It might be a poem wedged between their molars that they can neither swallow nor dislodge with a toothpick.

Living in New York, I might not have seemed so strange to my urban neighbors if they knew me, or to myself if I were ever introduced.

Every September brings changes. Every September I return to New York for a summer secretarial job that will defray college costs. September 1965, I begin graduate school at Columbia in Morningside Heights. The following year, I carry a welfare worker's black case book and head out on trains to visit my clients in slums around the city.

My unit supervisor is a relatively young black woman who smokes, drinks coffee, and chews gum simultaneously. She advises me to be cautious about adding prospective clients to the caseload of dependency. She is thrilled when I usher a rabbi through the application process to become a caseworker himself and leave the list of clients.

One day a client couple shows up in the welfare center. They parented many children, about eighteen. The guy stumbles in his usual drunken state. The woman is manic. She declares loudly that people have come to the center to kill them. We alert the police who evacuate those who have not yet run out in terror. Paranoia is proactive.

On another memorable day, I ordered separate bedding for a woman who was sleeping with her teenage son. Once I heard rats squeaking in the pipes as I climbed the urine-soaked stairs to another client. She was a young woman whose mother had either been burned out or died down South. The death reunited the unprepared newly arrived non-resident with her many illegitimate children. Her story was replicated by thousands. They occupied an apartment in a brownstone needing renovation near the Museum of Natural History. Disregarding my suggestion, she never took her kids to the museum.

I used my ability to order furniture, clothing, household appliances and school supplies to comply with the job description and to reward clients who cared for their kids. Truancy, neglect, the absence of father figures, and the incapacity of too many young women to mother their children proved the rule. The visits became unhappy reminders of what could happen to kids born into intergenerational hopelessness. Poverty was a perennial. That was one reason I wanted to teach black students. I thought I could help them break the cycle. The following year I began a 30-year career in which I enjoyed many successes and quite a few failures. It was worth the effort.

On many days while awaiting tests, results, and appointment as a teacher, I worked as a caseworker. I trudged through gritty snowbanks to ascend housing projects. On other gloomy winter days, I walked up the stairs in hallways darkened by shattered light bulbs. I would arrive to find my clients had cashed their checks to furnish trips to Puerto Rico. Upon returning, they simply reapplied for checks to reimburse them for stolen payments. Invariably the payments always reimbursed clients for checks that had been cashed. Clients avoided accountability and eviction for failure to pay their rent.

By that time radical professors Cloward and Piven directed "welfare rights" groups to overburden the welfare system. They demanded credit cards for clients to use in department stores. I had had enough scripted compassion.

Initially my supervisor seemed somewhat insensitive, but her innate conservatism protected people in temporary need from becoming permanent wards of the state. We worked well together. She appreciated my prompt and thorough reports, attention to my clients' needs, and commitment to putting in full days in the field when other caseworkers skipped out early.

Originally, I found myself more aligned with my fellow caseworkers. They were radicals with college degrees attesting to their ability to pass a simplified social worker exam. Members of a radical union faction, they were more interested in hook ups, sit-ins, and stopping the war in Vietnam. I had contempt for liberals who lived comfortably in the status quo with occasional corrective reforms.

I respected radicals who warred on complacency and comfort. We strove for revolutionary action. We demonstrated in synch until I discovered that they were anti-Israel. They devoted themselves to keffiyeh-topped demagogues. I confronted cracks in the Corinthian columns of my communist discipline.

After years of visits, the non-residence center replaced field work with appointments. That change coincided with my year's tenure. Clients were supposed to keep appointments to meet their case workers at the center. The end of site visits meant case workers never again saw their clients' homes, providing less insight into the family dynamics. The rising incidence of attacks on caseworkers occasioned the changes. The little black book no longer meant safe passage.

In the interim, the Board of Education processed my application and exams and deployed me to a Chelsea situated high school serving students from Harlem. As a youngster, I committed myself to teaching black students. I promised I would deliver the equivalent education I received as the fortunate beneficiary of several outstanding teachers. The less likely they were to attend college, the more important it was that they were well educated in high school. I commuted with my students on the A train to my classrooms located far from suburban N.J. I was home.

September always brings changes. In 1968, I began my teaching career in New York City, carrying out a resolution I made back in eighth grade. I taught thousands of black, Dominican, and Puerto Rican thousands. By the time I retired and said farewell to New York, it was September of 1998. My husband drove me to the Bronx to pick up my last paycheck as Assistant Principal. We headed west with the dog on my lap and our belongings piled in the van. I wore a small diamond and sapphire ring, the September birthstone, that my parents purchased for my sixteenth birthday. I wear it still.

In September, my aging dog had her last doomed litter of pups. Disease poisoned her milk, and the pups died one by one. I sat on the couch holding the palm-sized creatures, watching them shudder and expire. There was nothing I could do. I gave them the warmth of my fingers petting them. I hoped the sound of my pulse would comfort them. My dog died during my freshman year at college.

During my junior year, an unpredictable death shocked the entire nation.

I had just returned from an interview with the school of education. I entered the student center in time to hear a radio announcement. President Kennedy had been shot in Dallas. Then, the confirmation. He was dead. The college student center became a punctured tire emptying of air and students. The students all ran home for warmth and comfort. I do not know why I went home, too.

My parents experienced joy over the assassination. For them, JFK typified one more cold war warrior with a little glamor. I was stunned. I should not have been. I found there was nothing I could do. I was just one more puppy nursed on poisoned milk whose fate was sealed by accident of birth.

I had made a different mistake a few Septembers before my parents denied me a part in the national ceremony of mourning for JFK. Several Septembers earlier than college, I found a seat each day after classes in the lobby of the newly constructed high school. One of the most popular boys in the class was an athlete and class officer. He had an academic average that did not intimidate and an appealing smile that did. We would sit on the couch and talk and talk. Like most of our classmates, he was born in the city and found his way to the suburbs on time for our encounters. When his family turned him over to a NJ relative, he fled neglect and abuse in a tough neighborhood, Hell's Kitchen. Ryan landed in the refuge of an attic provided by a barely accommodating member of his extended family. Fortunately, he connected with caring neighbors who fed his body and intellect.

Perhaps he became a writer who carried the city in his pocket like so much loose change. Maybe he lived vampiric hours, turned his back on his own shadow and did not see his reflection. He might have walked through the walls of other peoples' hearts and sealed up his pain in a secret crypt. Fugitive from an abusive family, perhaps he waited for a fairy tale princess.

A metamorphosizing kiss might free the artist in his soul and enable him to write his own ending. But then, in September, the three o'clock sun was still warm and the evenings just beginning to chill like apple cider. Conversations with the boy who liked me but would never ask me on a date captivated me. As a Jew, I suspected that I lived on the wrong side of the religious river.

How wrong I was about everything.

We met up at a 50th high school reunion. Ryan confessed he feared asking me out. The product of any unhappy home life, he was mentored, fed, and rescued from an attic of obscurity by Jewish neighbors. He piloted a plane in Vietnam. A man possessed of a first-rate intellect, he led an interesting and meaningful life. He combined military commitments, business acumen, and a love of piloting his own plane into wilderness areas. He pursued a slew of hobbies including photography and racing cars as sleek as thoroughbreds. How fortuitous that we never dated! We became friends. Sometimes September had a happy ending.

One September, eons later, my older son almost died. Notice that I did not make it passive. I did not embroider old-fashioned words like "pass" or "depart." He asked me when he had already recovered, "Was I dying?" His harrowing question sliced through the silence.

I kept seeing Seth as a child. He developed his parents' love of nature on family trips to California where the gauzy scarves of sunset floated across the dunes of Torrey Pines. My dreams descended only to be swallowed in the throat of a wave. I watched foam retreat like a weary lover leaving the sand to cool. Profiled against the breakers, I saw my son's face, spray dazzled. Minutes later, the sun began to fall. He followed the current, toppled the crest, and crashed at my feet. He was the gift of past tides and the ceaseless churning of blood and salt.

The ocean has always challenged man with change. The Atlantic off Cape Cod morphed from inviting to hurricane crazed. The Pacific provided a playground for my child in San Diego. I saw him as he was then, a child unafraid to stand up to the surf.

Years later, my breath hides. It heats the pale-yellow globe of the surgeon's mask I affix, entering the isolation room at the local hospital. My son falls ill to a virus with no name. Tubes, needles, and the metronome of clear liquid pulse into his vein. His fever crests at high tide and all of him that is mine threatens to wash out to sea. Meningitis.

I cannot untangle the strands of kelp that attach to my limbs and pull me down. For weeks, I walk hallways littered like a beach with images of driftwood bleaching bone-white at midday. People I know pass in hospital corridors. We have coffee and do not speak. We freeze, each alone until the first chips of ice yield to Seth's teeth. Then his beard yields to a razor and his question pierces the silence. "Was I dying"?

While Seth smiles, my husband buys airline tickets to the beach of next summer. My son returns to work for his first veterinary job. I lift the salt-slick conch to my ear and hear that question rolling in and out with the tide. "Was I dying?"

"No," I answer. "No! It was never even a possibility."

I thank the doctors. The first appearance of a chunk of ice calves, diminishing my glacial atheism. I am not yet ready to thank God. I do so belatedly, acknowledging that I could do nothing to save my son. God and the doctors did that.

It is September again, and I wonder when pagan gods of a Marxist Pantheon will disappear. The Earth spins its way around the sun, doubling back on September. A defective dreamcatcher still swings from the rearview mirror of memory, jumbling glimpses of nightmares. The dreamcatcher snares them in the net, disturbing sleep. Sometimes, metronome mobile, the dreamcatcher syncopates the sweet vision of doe and fawn in the meadow. Occasionally, it captures the smiles that sway the heart and the spirits that soar on currents. Gradually, balance gets restored to times past and present.

Piñatas and cornucopias did not fill my childhood. My parents worshipped the Soviet Union and filled our rooms with Russian folk tales and nesting dolls. But sweet candy apples, an American treat, did not fill those years.

Years later they bought the same books and nesting dolls for my sons. They continued to praise the Soviet tyranny. They slammed the Jewish state. I pictured the Russian dolls decapitated in a marketplace in Tel Aviv. Mortality sat inside each nesting doll that encapsulated a smaller doll. A terrorist bomb turned the dolls into dust. The Soviet Union created the PLO. It radicalized the terrorists who bled Israel. It contributed to the slaughter of children, heedless of their birth right to enjoy books and toys. The precedent of their parenting foretold poor prospects for their ability to be loving grandparents.

Memory made me think of the ocean of decades enclosing smaller bodies of water and of time. I envisioned the lakes, puddles, tears, and amniotic fluid we had been. I reimagined moments, days, weeks, years and memorials. September stabbed at my sleep. I needed no charm bracelets to remember the births of my children.

Memory sets a table before me.

11

LEGACY

My own youth slips outside me, becoming a scepter I hold in my hands. I pass down a double-edged treasure. The legacy imparted to my sons offers the power to avoid repeating mistakes I made. I celebrate their birthdays with the candlelight of possibilities. I stretch a rubber band around the globe gathering bits of glacial brilliance and equatorial sands. Treasures invest majesty in promises kept. I try to bury prospects for mistakes and mistreatment in the catacombs. Laughter awaits liberation from the vault. I hand my children the key.

Dust motes swirl above ancient arguments. The commanding presence of all the missed opportunities brings me to my knees. In frozen forests of uncertainty, I ponder my response. Submission or supplication, it is one and the same. People I loved died. I keep them alive in memory. My parents died. I sort through the barbed words and brutal assaults they bequeathed to their children. I vow to throw them in the trash. This constitutes my spring cleaning.

Once I pushed my younger son in a stroller through the cornfields of the Amish country. On a summer evening Jake, raised his dimpled hand saying, "Reach up and touch the moon, Mommy." I could not do it. I could not pass on many things when I affixed the transponder to the windshield. I attached it just above the dreamcatcher, to try to make my sons' passage easier.

They must cross the desert without me, to find their own promised land.

I traveled with a dreamcatcher.

They travel with God.

One September, I was seated at the word processor preparing an evaluation of a teacher in my department. Suddenly, the phone rang. "You don't know me, but I'm your cousin Petra."

I had just turned fifty-two or three.

Sometimes, or oftentimes, exact dates or years don't matter.

My first cousin lived in Anne Arbor. Stalin's ghost sentenced us shortly after our respective births to live apart and unknown to each other for the next fifty years. We inhabited that strange gulag for golden, grieving souls who cannot connect. We were from separate orbits in Siberia living over the fault line of Marxist dialectic. Our fathers' estrangement sentenced us to be strangers.

Two first cousins linked by bad blood between our fathers lost out on family. We both found our way to Jewishness through the umbilical cord that stretches from future to past. We both waited for the death of our parents to free us to write. We remained wary of spit polish shine, avoiding euphemisms in describing the political schism. We delved eagerly into working the leather of our very personal history with words.

We laid wreaths of family photos on the coffin of the Cold War. Over the phone we wondered what the Freedom of Information Act had to say about reunions. We had both drunk the sacramental wine of civil rights like shots downed, straight up. We had both marched, demonstrated, signed petitions, and gone into teaching. The NYC Board of Education employed both of us.

We wondered which of our fathers betrayed the other. We resolved to cross the abyss.

Why did brotherhood in the abstract outweigh the shared youthful experiences of three brothers? One was apolitical, but the other two went from boyhood allies in the streets to lifelong enemies. Despite an eventual rift, they shared memories of two men who, as boys, had teamed up. They would hurl horseshit fresh from the delivery wagons at the hordes of Irish and Italian street toughs who early defined them both as Jews and underdogs. They both cast off the designation

"Jew" and held high the tag of "underdog." Both became communists.

For my father, it was a lifelong loyalty. For his brother, ideological devotion did not survive the communist terrorism and tyranny. He broke with the movement and quit the party when Stalin's perfidy was publicized for all to know. Petra's father, my unknown but much castigated uncle, ascended from lawless communism to study U.S. law. As a professor, he taught constitutional principles far removed from Marxism. The other, fine-tuning the ear of a recording engineer, was deaf to his brother, to his own children, and to our right to lay claim to our cousins.

Petra and I salvaged that bizarre legacy in the strange hours after the downfall of the Soviet Union. It took the death of her father, and the aging of my own, for us to free ourselves of their past. We found each other and a better future.

Petra came to New York with her family, and of course, they came to our house for dinner. Our other first cousin, Ronnie, son of the third of our father-brothers, arrived with his partner. And we three shone like fish scales gleaming in an Indian summer pond. Three cousins spoke simultaneously, exhibiting similar mannerisms. We embraced our newfound affection.

There were beams of discovery reminiscent of the jade, azure and purple flashes of lake waters plummeting from the shore to greater depths. Stories spilled with gossiping snowmelt into the confluence of private pasts and shared confidences. Slips of white foam edged over the granite of our fathers' mutual estrangement. Small truths bloomed in my small living room, and cousins separated by a paternal civil war reunited.

When I first heard Petra's voice, I still lived in a New Jersey town without charm. When I walked my dog, I imagined prickly pear cacti instead of familiar fire hydrants. I wanted to be far from where I was.

Three years ago, in September, I retired from the New York City Board of Education. I would do my hiking on the second half of the loop trail far from my unremarkable address. In that time, Petra and I have grown closer. My dog and my mother have died.

In Arizona they call the mountains that rise above the desert "sky islands."

Creations of altitude, they stand framed by forest. Nature's towers remained intact. The Twin Towers did not.

Since September 11, 2001, I have felt like a New Yorker in the Diaspora. My body lives in the Southwest, but my heart returns to the Northeast. Once again, I find myself attached to city grids by the umbilical cords of television, phone, and e-mail.

The "sky islands" of the World Trade Center imploded along with my illusions. A television interview introduced me to two volunteers at ground zero. Their perfect passion to rescue and recover magnified the accents I missed hearing. New York still smoked for weeks after the attack. A seven-month-old baby suffered from cutaneous Anthrax. Death surrounded me, and there was nothing I could do.

Determined to never forget, we send checks to charities to help veterans. We followed the war on terror, a silly name because terror is a tactic, not the enemy. Arriving at a community theater rehearsal I announce, "They got Zubaydah." I expect recognition of the name and applause for the achievement. No one responds.

This was not WWII. Many Americans seemed removed from events, just months after the chaos and carnage of a terrorist attack on the financial and military foundations of our republic. The layman did not move pins on homemade maps to track the progress of our troops. Too many of us did not familiarize themselves with the ideology that issued fatwas against our civilization. Too many of us did not realize that we were the infidels marked for death. Do-gooders slapped "Co-exist" slogans on their cars. They attended interfaith breakfasts with unvetted imams who delivered contradictory messages in English and Arabic.

Jihadism represents an existential foe. Americans impervious to the ideological menace suffer from attention deficit disorder and amnesia. In the Holy War against modernity, jihadists point out that Westerners have the watches, but they have the time.

I found it remarkable that I am learned to love the country my parents taught me to hate. They deprived me of a nation and family.

It struck me as strange that insomnia, the stalker of my adolescence, looked up my new address. It found me in Arizona on this side of September the eleventh. It seemed strange that I put aside my writing for weeks, waiting to see if there is anything I could do about the death all around me. And there was nothing I could do. Eventually, my husband and I found outlets to share our outrage, analysis, and research. We engaged in public speaking, distributing primary and secondary source materials documenting the scourge of jihadism. We disseminated wake up calls to our neighbors. Some responded to our presentations. Others hit the snooze button.

During one September, I was ill. My legs held me up no better than overcooked string beans. Food ran through me like the spring thaw on the Merced River. My head hovered, balloon tilting and helium congested. One enormous right eyelid collapsed like the Tokyo stock market. I imagined a stroke rather than just the flu had cancelled all communication with the visible world. Tawny lion sunlight swallowed my back. Sweat bubbled beneath the thin crust of skin. Suddenly, I succumbed to chill currents that moved like snakes across my earlobes and twisted down my neck to where a barricade of goose down held the line.

I recovered, of course, slightly off course. I stopped reaching so frequently for the solace of chamomile tea and tissues. But I have already been introduced to the sick old lady with dust-streaked hair and bones. I wondered if I would wear a desiccated face in the future, overlooking a horizon scraped with sagebrush that no moisturizer could replenish or restore my complexion.

Not even lightning's smile in late summer monsoon squalls could cause a flash flood of joy to alter my understanding of becoming old. I have seen what I will become. I understand what I have never been. I know now that I am crushed fingers in the door of my own decisions. I growl like a bear in a steel trap. One misstep relegates freedom to a memory. But what if I am wrong?

Bad choices are a sorry legacy. I write the obit for my youth instead of making plans for my future. I will look different, but my outlook will also be different. Growing old offers another opportunity to grow up. The time has come to spring the trap.

I lost interest in mirrors decades before I received a diagnosis of Multiple Myeloma. At age 81, I began to wear wrinkles like Girl scout badges.

Now, signs of aging attest to my survival.

Hurricane Carol blew through that distant August almost seventy years ago. That is when I started to write this memoir, if only in my mind. Waves of indifference rode in the hard, bright glitter of the sea. Decades passed like plankton through the baleen of a whale. Millions of microscopic memories moved on the currents and then they vanished. I have eaten my days. The tides have worn my rough edges smooth.

What was once clear turned translucent and then opaque. Only one week remains immutable, like a scarab ring. Sometimes, driving out of the circle commuting to the house where my children slept, studied, and played, I could smell Falmouth. I felt my saltshaker heart pour fresh tears to season the vanquished decades.

Shortly before I turned eleven, before anything was over, before much had begun, I picked up a sun-heated stone. When I threw it, the stone dropped, disappearing beneath the surface. I felt the sun's heat surrendering to the cold depths. My Falmouth family found death in the cold angry Atlantic. Yet again, I cried for them. I cried for me.

I reheat the poems of my refried dreams. Here, have some. Onyx tire inner tubes swirl in the roiling seas. Surf punishes the beach. Sand drowns in recrimination. My legs dangle rhetorically as I float. My eyelashes are sticky with salt. I blink back the tub of churned butter sunshine spilling down, alchemically coating spray and spittle with gold. I knew happiness in Falmouth and mostly misery in my parents' home.

I breathe and wipe away tears knowing I lived happily most of my life with my husband, my sons, my grandchildren. I loved relatives and friends who enriched my life for decades. Some died, and some wrote me off for political reasons. Many remain steadfast. I salvage the sweet memories of all those relationships.

Scab to scar without shape described the one momentous week I vacationed in childhood. I remember a firefly dance of evenings without end, sand dunes without shadows, cousins without a father, and me with a father I wanted to give away.

Remembered pain splinters the soul with green glass shards of coke bottles refashioned by the sea. The tweezer of maturity removes these splinters.

In our abused childhood, tears reworked weekends as my brother, sister, and I hunkered down in dark closets. We needed sutures rather than tweezers to repair us.

We hoped to outlast our father's fugitive temper and our mother's overcooked roast beef ventriloquism. She put words in our mouths so he could smack them from our faces. Like a tourist at an old castle, you could not miss their gargoyle altitude. They exhibited an all-seeing, know-nothing prominence. Their stony authority projected a façade of family. Our house concealed a front for insomniac dreams. It contained a font of unbidden salt streams.

At summer's end, everything ended. Only the exhaust pipe, remnant of the stove bottom remained, a souvenir of gravity. One week held its breath and expired before the last body washed up on the rocks with the seaweed along the bay.

My cousins, gone, along with my baby tooth stuck in the Sugar Daddy. Gone, my favorite aunt, talisman against the future of living forever with my parents. Gone, the chance of Cape Cod summer sanctuary every year. A perennial taste of paradise.

Gone, summer nights with sleep, the caboose trailing an endless train. Gone the susurration of waves, silenced by the roar of jetliners smashing into skyscrapers.

I think about the men and women who fell like dolls from one hundred and ten stories above the street. The years before and after September eleventh define my sons' calendars. The twin towers of tragedy and terrorism loom before and behind them. My nation looks out at the day through the smoke still lifting from the pit of lower Manhattan.

It is 2025, and September 11, 2001, recedes like a hairline into the past. But the day still lives, and we are still here. I have more to say. I added chapters at the suggestion of my younger son. Dear audience, keep turning the pages.

I outgrew and outlived my communist straitjacket. I found a way out of the closet where I hid surrounded by hand-me down clothes, escaping a dysfunctional childhood. Hurricane Carol had the power to blow down the steeple on Boston's Trinity Church. I rejected the relationship modeled by my parents. My marriage became stronger than theirs. It became stronger than the storm that toppled the steeple.

I reclaim what remains of my life, memories, family, faith, nation and civilization. There is still time.

12

BABY TEETH

In 2025, I can still recollect my sons' earliest words or endearing acts. I recall all the "firsts." They are preserved like Hollywood stars' footprints at Grauman's Chinese, or the heroes memorialized on Mount Rushmore. Visions of the first time either baby flipped himself over, sat, or stretched his arms up to be sprung from the confines of the crib endure. Floods of spilt milk and apple juice defied promised protections of sippy cups to prevent spills.

Lullabies and bedtime stories replete with perfected stalling tactics eventually lulled them into sleep. "I'm thirsty," or "I have to go to the bathroom," only delayed the inevitable. The first steps accompanied first words uttered in high pitched tones. Their vocal range lowered as they grew taller with the passage of time.

As I weaved between flexibility and consistency in parenting practices, I attempted to socialize my boys without breaking their spirit. The days that seemed to stretch forever began to gallop with the passing of the years.

My vivid recollections of their incredible encounters with life remain. No doubt my maternal love for them elevates the ordinary to the extraordinary. They ran into the ocean; I stayed in the shallows. Initially I relished all the ways in which they were unlike me. Later I rejoiced in what we shared as well. As a working mother, I figured out some ways to maximize our time together, which I share in this book.

Here are a few of those linguistic x-rays into their souls as they grew and flourished. They let me love them from the inside out.

I treasure their facility with language, their capacity to create, to synthesize, and to question. I treasure their ability to convey old adventures they retain from their childhood.

On any given morning, I would open the door to baby Seth's room to find him seated in his crib "doing his homework." He would repeat any new word he had just learned. In his infant seat in a nearby restaurant, he pointed up to the ceiling calling out, "light, light up there." On other days, he sat himself on the rug between two toy pianos, playing one with each hand.

We knew then that piano lessons would figure in his future. We did not foresee that a Russian emigree, a piano teacher of gifted students, would take him on to polish talent with technique. She invited him to live with her family when they moved to California. We declined to give him up.

Years later, another piano teacher, responded to an interview covering her lengthy career as a piano teacher. She was a student of the founder of the Julliard School. She took us to task, lamenting the fact that she finally discovered a prodigy after decades of teaching, only to have his parents buy him a puppy and lose him to a career in veterinary medicine.

As Seth grew, his interest in the "M" words, music, medicine, and the military deepened. His love of his son Marc, whose first name began with an "M," topped his passions and priorities. Occasionally he plays a classical piece for me. More often he entertains as lead vocalist of rock cover bands, displaying keyboard talents or playing a flute riff. My husband bought me a keyboard to help me survive isolation during coronavirus shutdown times. After years of daily disappointment playing simplified classical and popular pieces, I confirmed that my son's talent owes nothing to inheritance.

I took Jake to a county park on days when I drove my older son to Hebrew School. I directed him to get dirty. A child chastened to keep his clothes and hands clean cannot be expected to have fun. When his session with the playground was over, we got back into the car to pick up his brother. He told me he was thirsty, but he acknowledged that "of course, there is no milk in the glove compartment, so I will open the window and drink the wind."

When he arrived home one day, he went to the sink to wash his hands. Jake proclaimed, "I am turning on a winter of cold water and a summer of hot water to make spring" in the single faucet. The little boy in railroad engineer striped Oshkosh overalls I strapped into his car seat showcased his gift as a poet.

Both boys learned to read when they were two years old. Jake took his favorite book, "Babar Comes to America" to kindergarten for show and tell to read to his class. On an open school night, I asked his teacher if he had had an opportunity to read to her. She dismissed my interest, explaining that she had to teach the class their letters.

But Jake and I spent many rewarding hours sitting on the front porch steps with beloved library books that were checked out time after time. *One Eyed-Jake* recounted pirate adventures. *Roberto and the Bull* told the tale of a Spanish child. *The Wild Whirlwind* and *Where the Wild Things Are* lingered for years as a valued part of his private, personal book collection. We played games of whiffle ball in the backyard as he outdistanced the hedges growing taller around us.

Seth read many of the classics, including from Jules Verne and other authors beloved by kids for generations.

When my sons reached the age for day camp, I assigned a reading hour. After socializing all day, they needed to spend some time alone, in the company of books. After a day of camp activities, barbecues, and an exhausting bus ride home, they arrived with sun-smeared faces and dirty towels.

Both sons read books about history, prejudice, and war. They played piano, and I reluctantly purchased video games for their enjoyment contingent upon reading and practicing. Years later, Jake confessed he appreciated having had to earn the video games.

Sometimes, the lesson I tried to teach ended up teaching me a lesson. Parents too must balance flexibility and consistency. Sometimes my decisions succeeded and other times they failed to maintain the balance. I emerged from some dilemmas uncertain of my decisions.

One day, Seth called out from the living room. An upset little boy stopped his piano practice. Busy fixing dinner in the kitchen, I always found his practice sessions resembled a concert rather than a rehearsal. He made so few mistakes. I went to him to ask what was wrong. He told me "Mozart never made a mistake."

Another time, he got off the bus from a private country day school in tears to tell me he had not learned anything new that day. He was a perfectionist, forgiving his mother's mistakes, but toughest on himself. He always set high standards for himself. He did not compete with others. He worked to meet his expectations for himself. Seth also studied the flute and the oboe.

Jake's cello teacher gave me a rave report on his progress, remarking that he must practice a lot. In fact, he did not practice cello at all. He simply "transposed" what he learned from piano lessons to the new instrument. I kept his secret. In deciding between violin and cello, he selected cello because he preferred the lower, darker notes. Seth's Russian teacher was eager to enlist Jake in her troop of promising piano students.

While very young, they played with an armada of toy boats. Sailing their miniature fleets, they alternated singing back jazz riffs I sang to them. On vacations, they sang and harmonized to songs on the radio of rental cars. Seth often sang with a band. My Aunt Ann sang opera professionally. Their paternal grandfather had a melodious voice. My husband and I filled our house with music. It took.

On trips, they wow audiences with their singing contributions at karaoke or a piano bar. Throughout my life, music and my sons added harmony. The discordant noise of my childhood dissipated. The lyrical chords of a loving husband and sons replaced the roars of awful parents.

Every trip to a grocery store presented an immersion in shapes, sizes, colors, numbers, and letters. It offered "Sesame Street" without a television. During a particular food shopping excursion, Seth suddenly stopped in the middle of the cereal aisle to request, "Mommy, tell me the story again about the daddy lion and the mommy lioness and how they make a baby lion cub." Other shoppers' carts screeched to a stop as they leaned in to hear my answer.

Jake recited world geography trivia on the days I drove him to the orthodontist. He ventured from continents to countries, oceans to rivers and lakes, and capitals to exports. One summer vacation to a national park in the Sierras, Jake warned us to stop looking for a bear that had been spotted outside a lodge. We were making our way along an enormous fallen log across a wildflower-quilted meadow. "The bear will eat me first because I'm the littlest." We could not disagree and turned back. Our sons learned about the world and the ways of the wild.

During a stay at the Wawona Hotel near the giant groves section of Yosemite, we watched a mother raccoon lead her troop of babies across a railing. They were searching for an accessible garbage can. Jake beat me in chess which we played on the porch in the evenings after a dunk in the tank. The cavernous tank washed away the dust and dirt of a daily hike in a deep and chilling swimming pool.

A herd of territorial deer visited the tank, which was set on the front lawn and surrounded by tall trees. The deer invested in a time share of sorts, returning to the rustic resort at dusk each day. Years later, an idiot shot them all. Those beautiful creatures still live in memories and in a painting my sister gave us.

Seth made money in his first gig. He played some piano tunes by heart on the instrument available in the main "living room" after dinner. A ranger placed a glass jar on the piano for tips. Other guests, delighted by a little boy with musical talent, dropped in coins and bills. Seth purchased a Swiss army knife. That was the magic of Mariposa Grove.

On another occasion, Seth used his funds to buy matching dolphin pins for his father and mother as a thank you for a visit to Mission Bay, California. I have that dolphin pin. I plan to be buried with it and with a poem written by Jake, and with the wedding band my husband placed on my finger so many decades ago. Some things you cannot leave behind.

As a young mother raised on the left, I refused to let my sons play with guns. I embraced the bloodiest ideology in history, communism, but objected to toy guns. Clambering over boulders high in the Sierras, my sons retrieved large branches to joust with each other. While the sun heated the space between my skin and my clothes, and the boys sweated into the sun-bleached light, I realized that the instinct to fight is innate. My boys did what comes naturally.

That moment of illumination required many additional micro-epiphanies to mature into a clear-headed endorsement of the Second Amendment. The testosterone driven core of masculinity blesses us with partners and sons who provide for us and protect us.

On a vacation to Host Farm in Pennsylvania Amish Country, I was pushing Jake's stroller through the cornfields while the moon rose high in the sky. He pointed up and said, "Mommy, reach up and touch the moon." Mornings in the Rockies, my husband and I left the boys sleeping in a toasty, heated cabin to take a 5-mile trek to the river. It was our time. We could not touch the moon, but we could say "yes" to other requests our sons made. Usually early risers, sometimes they wanted to sleep. That worked.

We did not speak as we made our way out of West Yellowstone along the meandering Madison. After a luxuriant stretch in the sunlight, we returned to the cabin to fetch the boys and indulge in pancakes at our favorite local breakfast place.

In Rocky Mountain National Park, a precocious pre-teen, Jake, asked his father about the elk. Sporting an impressive rack of antlers, an elk bugled his intentions while rounding up prospective mates from the interface between the meadow and the forest. Aspen leaves jingled like wind chimes in the crisp Autum air. Len explained the mating ritual. Jake was impressed that one male was able to secure his status as stud. "How can I get a job like that some day?" he wondered.

As a teacher, I frequently arrived at school to find Fisher-Price toys in my pocket. I took Seth to school with me when he was still a toddler. We rode the A train. In the classroom of an old building in Chelsea, home to students from Harlem who commuted with me on the subway, Seth drew a freehand sketch of Indonesia on the board. He asked students to take out their notebooks. He explained rice cultivation on terraced mountain sides. Years later, he took his native teaching skills into his medical and military careers.

On another occasion, both boys gave lectures on dinosaurs from their strollers at the Museum of Natural History. They distinguished between herbivores and omnivores while identifying each giant skeletal model. As a veterinarian, Seth visited my leadership classes to answer questions about college from students who were often the first in their families to attend.

Jake and one of his friends attended a couple of Saturday workshops I offered my high school students to explore various subjects with kids from totally different backgrounds. No strict boundaries between my own family and my students existed. My sons moved like elk from the sequestered forests of suburbia to the metropolitan meadows of NYC.

My husband helped facilitate cultural interactions with intervisitations. Students from suburban NJ high schools, both blue collar and affluent communities, spent days at my NYC high school with minority students. My students, black and Latino, visited the suburban JN high schools as well for a day of leadership training. As anticipated, despite trepidations about preconceived notions, the NJ kids and NYC kids concluded that people were people. Dr. King's admonition to judge people based on the content of their character rather than the color of their skin stood my sons and my students in good stead. I hope such experiences protected them from the political correctness and reverse racism that poisoned society for decades to come.

If these anecdotes jostled your memory, good. No doubt all parents have fond memories of their children's development and achievements. Why not tell them how much you treasure them? Why not share the memories with others?

My sons subsequently chose college roommates with "diverse" backgrounds without ever engaging in self-loathing assumptions or stereotypes. They never checked off boxes. They never fell for cultural Marxism and its malevolent erasure of individualism.

13

MEMORIES BEYOND A LIFETIME

I did not record memories of my sons' words or experiences in any order. Sequence is irrelevant. What survives are the moments filled with syllables that still speak to me. Some say that children are the price we pay for grandchildren. Loving a child one umbilical cord removed proved easier. My grandson, Marc, continues to delight.

We took him hiking in Shenandoah National Park when he was seven or eight. Walking along a hot, dusty trail, he commented that sometimes bad things happen. They can be caused by nature like a volcano, earthquake, or tsunami. They can be manmade disasters, like war. But then, he continued, sometimes things are perfect. The earth moves at the right distance from the sun. Too close it would burn up. Too far away and the cold would be inhospitable to human life. Marc concluded that the earth on its axis and its orbit is perfectly positioned. And that, he ventured, manifests the work of God. For a grandmother raised as a communist, he philosophized more than a stunning reflection. It was a revelation.

Before he entered kindergarten, Marc accompanied us to Vancouver to watch pods of whales breaching the waters surrounding our boat. He bravely sampled croissants and calamari for the first time. An avid hiker, he explored Stanley Park with its totems and scenic grandeur. He walked for miles, stopping only for snacks on park benches along the route to watch sea planes and yachts maneuver.

Leaving the hotel in the elevator one morning, he introduced his grandparents to the strangers riding with us. He explained that he might become a paleontologist, someone who studies dinosaurs, and offered smiles all around. An outgoing, adventurous and loving grandson, he travels with us today.

In an anecdote I call "economics by the scoop," Marc shared his theories of supply and demand at a local dairy. He did not yet learn the word "economics", but he figured out how the farm secured its profits. He said it was large enough to produce enough ice cream to attract buyers. It was small enough to manage to contain costs. The dairy cows lived on the property along with the facilities to manufacture and sell ice cream. The combination of prices and quality of the product attracted a loyal clientele. It was a family business whose brand and reputation were interchangeable.

The company relied primarily on its own resources to produce and profit from ice cream sales. Costs were relatively low. Marc realized that they could afford to make less profit per item if they had sufficient volume to meet their goals. They could make more profit per purchase if they raised their prices but might then risk lowering sales.

Beyond selling potholders and a one-time lemonade stand, I had no experience with business. A large NY bank did hire me one summer to report on how branch bank employees interpreted and implemented policies, rules and regulations. But my knowledge of economics awaited immersion in Thomas Sowell. I never grasped the principles of private property and capitalism the way my grandson did.

Charge too much and lose customers. Charge too little and undervalue your product. By having the cows and facilities right there, they did not have to spend a lot on transportation. By developing a boutique brand, they did not have to spend a lot on marketing. By controlling growth, they maintained a steady customer base. They did raise prices in the intervening years, but Marc recognized that those increases were reasonable and never interfered with a winning formula. Our astute grandson figured out the formula that let this small business thrive.

Most kids Marc's age would have been content with choosing which flavor or flavors to have. They would have focused on whether to order a sugar cone or a cake cone or whether sprinkles and whipped cream should top the sundae or shake. Marc's observations made him a wonderful companion. His commentaries on special events, family vacations, and informal get-togethers have made memories of moments spent with him the cherry on top.

Seth, Jake, and Marc moved on with recitals and concerts, games and graduations, girlfriends and marriages, achievements and adversities. I know that if you do not cut your kids' toenails, teach them to tie their own shoelaces, ride a bike, roller skate, or read and explore, you will not know them. If you do not drive them to religious classes and welcome their friends into your home, you will not bond.

If you do not involve them in painting the interior of their house, or in planting a garden for vegetables in the back yard, you risk missing out. If you do not respect their autonomy while demanding that they respect their parents, you fail to prepare them for the future.

We were fortunate to acquire two terrific "step" granddaughters. Despite the trials of divorce, we managed to remain a family. As the girls traveled from early childhood when we met them to adulthood, they extended their affection to grandparents who reciprocated. We credit our sons with fostering connections. After Seth's divorce from Marc's mom, the three children, now young adults, continue to bless our lives.

Parenting at a distance did not offer the same perspective or opportunities available to stay-at-home moms. I worked outside the home and loved my students. I worked inside the home. I devoted every minute possible to pursuing that elusive goal of providing "quality time." I realized that as a working mother, I deprived my children of some of the comfort and security that comes with a stay-at-home mom.

Children pay a price for feminist rationalizations, and for confiscatory taxes that require two incomes.

I provided an imperfect model of a woman who tried to do it all. I never scheduled time or money for me at the expense of my sons. We roller skated twice a week. I prepared dinner every night, drove them to all their activities and, inadvertently, gave them some space by not always being there. What better legacy could I claim than my children? They exceeded my expectations. They surpassed what I managed to give them. They manage to be their own men while remaining my sons.

Opportunities always exist to interact with your children. Sitting in a waiting room, taking a walk on a crisp autumn day, or going to the grocery store to buy milk multiply chances to do things together. You communicate while enlisting them in chores like painting their rooms, making "fast-food" style hamburgers, or supervising a school project. That might be all the time you have and all the time you need.

Going without some "treats" facilitates a way to teach anticipation, gratitude, and recollection. We rarely ate out and managed to survive in a house with one-and-a-half bathrooms. Only the bedrooms benefitted from air conditioning in summer with heat-busting window units. We had the necessities but little in the way of luxuries. Residents of a blue-collar suburban community, they both had friends who had more and friends who had less.

Our sons endured the anti-intellectual bullying and peer pressure that hooked some of their peers on conformity and other drugs. The boys managed to perform well academically despite the consequential pressures that pervaded our community.

They developed a code of conduct. Seth, subjected to brutal harassment, years later enlisted in the military, eventually volunteering to deploy to Iraq. Jake developed an uncanny ability to detect authenticity that helped him in later life. They respected individual integrity, not status. They developed character in the crucible of a crushing conformity.

We managed to provide a piano, lessons, and vacations out West where we introduced our boys to pristine views and a chance to share wildlife habitats. Ironically, they felt safer sharing remote areas with bears, wolves, and mountain lions than they did at school. That Seth fulfilled his childhood desire to become a veterinarian and marine biologist surprised no one who knew him. That Jake developed into a man who prioritizes faith and devoted himself to his principles and family, regardless of the cost, surprised no one who knew him.

Both developed an interest in martial arts, as had their father. Seth and his son Marc earned third degree black belts until the coronavirus lockdown in the early 2020s ended that shared hobby. Jake continues doing workouts to this day. They keep fit for their health and to defend themselves and others. How far have we come from those halcyon days when I thought I could protect them by denying them toy guns! Somewhere along the line, we must all grow up.

A persistent malignancy during my childhood taught some of my Christian counterparts that Jews were guilty of deicide. Significant changes, particularly in the Catholic Church, corrected that blighted belief. In Arizona, I researched ties between the Passover Seder and The Last Supper for a Catholic friend whose church was conducting a "hybrid" service. I discovered that many of my school friends were Catholics who adhered to faith. They had never been bigots.

Throughout my life, many of my closest friends have been Christians. In the spiritual void of the post-modern, post-Christian era, vile cults filled the void. The anti-religious diatribes of professional communists and jihadists grated on my ears. I increasingly embraced the Judeo-Christian tenets that undergird Western Civilization.

I am grateful for the Protestant and Catholic clergy and laity who embrace America and Israel. I am also grateful for the practitioners of Islam and all faiths who seek to match faith with modernity, rationality, and life-affirming traditions. I cherish ties to my fellow Jews who advocate for America and Israel.

My parents taught me to hate Christianity. In the aftermath of 9/11, a Protestant minister who had become a friend welcomed Arizona neighbors to a special commemoration. "The Battle Hymn of the Republic" echoed through the church. A few years later, he welcomed me with my two young Christian granddaughters to a Christmas service. That ecumenical spirit overtook my inherited antipathy for spiritual people who prayed for peace. I kept learning how wrong my parents and I had been.

If something in my memoir comforts a reader, then I am content. You can survive an awful, dysfunctional childhood and move through the world obsessed with your wounds. Instead of carrying the burden of bitterness, you can thrive with love. You can rely on the passage of time, reflection, and research for enlightenment. Determine not to let the negative outweigh the positive!

Dante recounts the trek. He circumvents the perilous Inferno. He circumnavigates the indeterminate stay in Purgatory. He journeys with hard-won wisdom to Paradise. Faith bestows power. Platitudes and Hallmark greeting card sentiments cannot convey the message on which the soul feeds. Faith facilitates progress to the confluence of two loves, for God and family.

Our ability to resurrect memories of joy and wonder empowers us. We can emblazon the dark night of fear with beacons of light.

The Old and New Testaments and the Ten Commandments exhort us to live in accordance with God's law. Ethics demand that we eschew evil. Every treasured memory, every reminder of our children's baby teeth, heals with a soothing antidote to pain and despair. In the search for meaning, memory serves a vital role. It connects us to smiling synapses.

Sometimes it seems that words are not enough. Life can be rough. Like the particle of sand in the oyster's shell, it causes a luminous pearl to surround it. Cliches and truisms exist because they capture something of the universal experience and of human nature. Words, however simple and straightforward, can be a stepladder leading from despair to happiness and hope.

Watch children for lessons in humility that life insists on teaching. They strive to become independent. They accept falling as the price for learning to walk on their own. They master application of language to gain some purchase and control over their lives, to test themselves, and learn new things. They are designed to be participants, not spectators paralyzed by fear, sloth, or failure. The goal of self-reliance drives them. In my experience as teacher and parent, agency is the antidote to passivity.

Children delight in music and movement. They want to be accepted, and they want to act alone. Their failures feed successes. They are unfinished even after you clear hurdles of your old age. You hold them in your arms and watch amazed as they grow to hold you at arm's length. Later they return as competent, caring adults to enfold you in family. They gift you with grandchildren. I wear a virtual charm bracelet with a clasp that links their childhood commentary to my heart.

14

LEN, MY LOVE

How do I introduce you to my love? Let me start with a crazy quilt of anecdotes. When he visited our sons at college, he greeted them or said good-bye with bear hugs. Their roommates, unaccustomed to demonstrations of affection, started to line up to receive their hugs. It became "a thing." When our older son's word processor died the day before a paper was due, Len ran out to buy a replacement and raced down the Turnpike to deliver it right on time. When he took headshots of actors for community theater productions, he would tell them, "Pretend you like me." They would immediately break into natural, ear-to-ear smiles. He enabled people to look good and feel good.

He felt sufficiently secure to indulge in a little self-deprecating humor. He charmed people with his warmth and wit. When he wore a bull riding t-shirt, he assured colleagues he had ridden bulls. Asked where he was from, he would claim participation in the witness protection program.

Receptive to the needs of others, his empathy elicited many private, personal revelations from colleagues. We called that "putting out the shingle" as though he were a professional therapist. Years later, recipients of his generous hospitality remembered visits to our home as high points in their lives.

Driving anywhere in our car, Len would put on music and often sing. He exhibits a pleasant voice and decent range, but his smiles remain the best part of his concerts on the road. The laugh lines crinkling around his profiled eye warm my heart.

For Hanukkah and Christmas shopping for our blended family, he would take the grandkids to the mall and let each one pick an item of clothing. Over time, he replaced toys and clothes with experiences. They learned to choose. He taught them that buying a lot of small things all the time would make it impossible to save for the big things. Trips would occur less frequently. They learned to postpone gratification of pleasure, a life lesson many adults fail to master.

An honest man, he drove back to a grocery store in Colorado to pay for an unchecked item. Sneaker laces somehow went unnoticed among the bags in the cart. One day he spotted a wad of bills on a pathway. He went to the zoo administrators to report the money and ask if anyone had claimed a loss. Len pointed out a waitress's mistake to her when she unintentionally rang up the bill that shortchanged the restaurant by a sizable amount. Len pointed it out so that she could correct it. He did not make a big deal about small acts of kindness and honesty.

Our younger son embarked on an American odyssey. Driving to distant places across the country, he entered a mileage marathon competition with his father. They would call each other from the road to report on scenery, weather, meals, and mileage. Each one aspired to best the other. Who could drive more hours in a single day? Len drove a straight 24 hours from Boulder to Bakersfield. Jake drove for fewer hours and covered fewer miles. But he dismissed his dad's achievement because Len traveled with me, whereas he drove alone. Today on road trips, they alternate driving with the three of us in the same car.

Len displayed great compassion every time he accompanied me for a blood test. I was so squeamish that he had to distract me with silly chatter. He complimented me on my faux courage. He saved my life the day I suffered a stroke, rushing me to the hospital for immediate medical attention. My inability to remember the names of Len's deceased parents and my increasingly garbled speech alerted him to the severity of the affliction.

He cried with me the next morning when my speech and memory miraculously returned. I did not need physical therapy. I required new medications, the implanting of a loop recorder to monitor my heart, and my husband.

From the emergency room, I accidentally frightened children when I almost struck out with a stroke. Apparently, I screamed incoherently until they took me inside for tests and procedures. I thought I was on a gurney weaving around sharp turns while I got wheeled to an MRI. I thought people were pushing me into hell. I remember saying, "I love you, Len." Maybe I said it in my mind.

Later that night, I regained some memory and could recall the birth dates of family. My full faculties for speech returned by the morning. I endured three panic attacks in the aftermath of the stroke. Visions of a claustrophobic descent into death alarmed me. Anxiety abruptly cut off sleep. My most recent MRI, taken last month, showed that my brain was fine. The neurologist's report took my age into account. I credit Len, God, my sons, and doctors with my recovery.

It seems strange that since I heard about my Multiple Myeloma, I have not had a panic attack. I experienced terror when my primary doctor introduced me to my disease. I cried in shock. Fear that time was running out and that an awful death seemed imminent pierced my equanimity. I cried as the impact of the diagnosis separated me from everything and everyone that tied me to my life.

The diagnosis sucker punched me. But I have not cried for myself since. I cry when I think about children with cancer. When a cop is murdered, I surrender to tears. Monthly contributions to charities for our warriors help assuage the tears. I cry, as I did all my life, when beautiful scenery or music moves me. I find myself saying, "I love you, Len," several times a day. Sometimes I tell him. Sometimes I say it in my mind. Sometimes, I include it in a prayer.

My heart pounded like the wings of a caged bird, flapping against the bars when I heard my Multiple Myeloma diagnosis on December 16, 2024. Len went into action, arranging for me to meet with a specialist the very next day. Since that time, he drives me to and from my treatments, prepares meals rich in protein for me, and encourages me with every promising lab test result. He does his best to mask any anxieties he cannot allay.

We pray together every night. He fills my days with gifts of reassurance, and patience. He books cruises, justifying the expense by stating, "You are happy at sea." He restricts a few sailings to the two of us. He schedules others for the family. Walking the decks, watching the seas and skies, searching for birds and dolphins, and gorging on buffets bolster my optimism. I hope the cruises provide him with some respite for the burden of prolonging my mortality that he has taken on.

Our best moments find us seated on the couch, my hand cuddling his head and neck. His presence, our prayers, my doctor, and our family constitute my strength. They are the flying buttresses that support my weight and help me stand. A cane helps too.

We married twice. We married secretly 61 years ago, and publicly, 60 years ago. "In sickness and in health," describes this stage of my life. Our appreciation for the time we have with each other continues to deepen. We still do a slow dance in the kitchen to songs we love. We met dancing. Still, dancing, even when sitting down, persists as my preferred exit strategy.

Before our wedding, I tried to teach Len the waltz. He refused to learn it. He turned out to be a good dancer, but one who could not be choreographed. He did a mean lindy, a kick ass twist, and a salacious version of dirty dancing. He provided a fitting tribute to Motown movements, particularly those of The Temptations. We met dancing in the finished basement of a high school friend. We hardly spoke all evening, but something spoke to my heart as I leaned against his hard chest and measured a slow dance enfolded in his arms.

My friends told me to watch him play basketball at the local Temple basketball court. I refused to pursue a guy, even a cute one, by watching sports. I started out a bit of a snob. That was one of many stupid attitudes he changed.

My parents signed on as libertines when it came to Marxist sanctioned relationships. But when it came to their children's sexuality, they presented themselves as Puritans. Not for us the unsupervised freedom of communist summer camps or international youth conferences. My mother in particular left me with chronic discomfort in my own skin.

My body rendered me vulnerable to visibility and rejection. My parents resented my dating anyone, unless it was a fellow attendee at a Pete Seeger songfest outdoor picnic. They would have reviled the young man who showed an interest in me had they known he described himself as a Trotskyite.

One night they let me invite Len to dinner. It turned out more like "an interview with the vampire." When Len seated himself at the head of the table, my father grew irate. Like the Camelot furniture, a round table occupied most of the dining room. Yes, my father got mad at Len for sitting at the head of a round table.

Another time, my parents invited Len's parents to their 25th wedding anniversary at their house. That sounds promising. But they did not include their son in the invitation. My crafty parents instituted a power play to force his parents to submit to their disrespectful summons. They attended. They hoped to improve the relationship. Their hope died in vain. Panning for gold in an area seeded with pyrite would have proven itself a better investment.

No prospect of rapprochement presented itself. Even after our public wedding, our respective sets of parents despised each other. Mine never relinquished the need to assert control, destroy their opponents, and establish ideological supremacy. Sick with an ism that infected them like a parasite, they hated Len's normal parents.

My parents loved humanity in the abstract and hated individual humans in the flesh. Years later, my mother repeatedly lamented that the Chinese did not kill more dissidents in the bloody aftermath of the Tiananmen Square Massacre. Len emerged as everything they were not. They were easy to loathe. Len was easy to love.

Over the years, the appeal of communism altered. Len's appeal did not change. Indeed, it grew as he taught me about love. We married secretly one summer when my parents threatened to throw me out. I had completed my junior year at college. Despite grades that improved every semester, they argued that I had to stop seeing him or I would never finish my education.

We took obligatory blood tests at a local hospital. We joined two of Len's buddies who served as our witnesses. We recited the traditional vows for the old judge in his dim-lit office. Our love never jeopardized my education. My parents did that. Sure enough, a few weeks later, my parents kicked me out.

I rented a room from a widow. Her husband had drowned in the sinking of the Andria Doria when it collided with the Stockholm. I commuted to NYC for a summer job. A telephone interview with the young CEO secured the job. A summer cold lowered my voice from soprano to the sexy alto he hired. My secretarial skills elicited attention and esteem.

The VP of the company took a lunchtime walk with me. He encouraged me to go to college. That presented the auspicious moment to tell him that I would be returning to college in a few weeks. I gave him notice. He asked me out. I gave him notice that I was married. Back at college, I fixed the President up with my roommate. She had a lower voice than I. We were all young. I could type 90 wpm. I had Len. It would all work out.

That salary combined with a campus job as secretary to the History Department. The college granted me the status of an emancipated minor. That qualified me to take out loans and enabled me to complete my degree. I was awarded a Woodrow Wilson Fellowship to earn a master's degree at Columbia University. In the following years, we managed to pay off that portion of my loans I could not work off by teaching in New York City. Teaching disadvantaged students earned some loan forgiveness.

The Fellowship paid for a master's, but I never hung the diploma. The ideological reality of Columbia's fall from intellectual grace became increasingly clear. My connection to that school became a source of mortification.

But in 1966, the Fellowship that covered the cost of a degree also furnished a stipend. With Len paying the bills, we used it to take our first road trip out West.

We visited friends in southern California, Sam and Daphne, after stopping at the Continental Divide. We consumed bagels at midnight in Las Vegas. Len drove 1,000 miles in 24 hours straight. We ended up in Bakersfield, where we devoured steaks and baked potatoes. I drove a total of one hour across a stretch of Nevada desert patrolled by airplane and posting no speed limit. I invited Len to take a nap or relax while I drove. He typically replied, "when you're driving, I'm not relaxing." He was right, and that remained the case for the following decades.

Len had better reflexes and mastered the art of defensive driving. He would drive for hours while I would tire after one. Fortunately, our Rambler had a front seat that lowered all the way back. Len outfitted the car with water bag contraptions to cool the air in lieu of air-conditioning we could not afford. Those features enabled me to snooze comfortably as we crossed the country.

After our public wedding, we rented a small apartment. Our friends Hailey and Lee, lived above. The four of us strengthened the ties of college acquaintanceship. Our friendship endured for a lifetime. We bought cheap balcony seats for the opera or a play a couple of times a year. My girlfriend and I would wear our one special NYC dress on those occasions. The four of us ordered venison, snails, and onion soup at Luray's French Restaurant. We saved enough from our $20 weekly food budgets to afford bagels and lox on the weekend.

The four of us eventually traveled to Europe in 1967 to explore five countries in a few weeks. For $5 a day, we reserved rooms in pensions with public bathrooms down the hall, bus tours of major cities, and the world at our fingertips. It was the first of many trips we took together. Our friendship began in college and intensified after we graduated, married, and moved into the same garden apartment complex. I finally managed to free myself officially from my parents, although liberation had begun with the first day of college.

Driving down to college my freshmen year, I found a sanctuary from an awful home situation. I met Len, already a junior, when I was sixteen. During summers, we went to the Village on hot summer evenings with Len's friend, a theater major. We sang folk songs as we crossed the George Washington Bridge. We listened to Symphony Sid's jazz show and Alison Steele, the Night Bird on the radio. Jazz and folk music coursed through out veins and molded our sympathies.

Following Len to the same college, we went to dances at the student centers and big fraternity parties. We had no money but had great times, making out at Passion Puddle, hanging around with friends, and occasionally breaking up only to get back together again.

In 1967, the four of us college buddies packed our bags and left New Jersey for London. Upon arrival, I committed one of those blunders that almost got us banished from Britain. It must have given Len cause to rethink his decision to marry me twice. When the official asked us why we had come to England, I quipped, "I came to be crowned queen." We came close to being banned.

There we stood in our trench coats with suitcases and cameras looking for all the world like what we were, American tourists. "I could keep you out. You might be crazy," the official commented despairingly. "I am crazy but not dangerous crazy," I countered. Perhaps he was close to a tea break or a nervous breakdown, but he let us through. After that, Lee and Len threatened to gag me, restrain my hands in cuffs, and otherwise intimidate me into silence, when we went through customs. It did not work.

Years later, Len and I flew to Tucson with our younger son to visit the University of Arizona. It was a cool night in February. After dinner at Carlos Murphy's and before walking over to the Opera to see *Turandot*, Jake and I went to the car to get our jackets. We left Len sitting in the lobby of a big hotel. While we were gone, two men accosted him. They asked for his identification. He asked for theirs. They were U.S. Marshals. They explained that he fit the description of a man involved in a drug deal. At that critical moment, we returned.

I volunteered that I had never seen that man, Len, before in my life. It was another moment of poor judgment and tertiary indiscretion. It was not the end.

I disclose these examples of my inappropriate behavior to illustrate Len's remarkable forbearance. That trip to Arizona constituted our first winter vacation. It convinced us that upon retirement, we wanted to live out West.

15

SEA CHANGES

Shortly after 9/11, Len and I drove from our retirement home in Arizona to Texas for our older son's graduation from a military officer course. It seemed like days, not hours, of driving to cross West Texas. We passed oil rigs and wind turbines dotting the expanses of ranch land and scrub. We had the best fajitas ever in Las Cruces, New Mexico, and rented a room at the officers' quarters on the base. Celebrating our son's accomplishments provided an adventure in Texas. Yahoo!

Seth got free tickets from a fellow veterinarian involved in marine biology who worked at the local Sea World. He invited several of his colleagues from the base. Len removed the back seats from the van to make room for them. On the way back, they were clustered on the floor of the van.

Given the high level of alert, the base was on lockdown.

The armed MP asked how many passengers were in the van and collected identification. While Len handed over the drivers' licenses, I informed him that there were more people hiding in the back.

Sometimes my idea of an element of levity borders on the insane. Fortunately, the MP did not shoot or arrest me. Len was used to my inappropriate antics, but Seth was chagrined. I provided one more opportunity for my husband and son to forgive me for occasional foolishness. I had become more circumspect by the time

I met some Gold Star families in Arizona. I conducted myself more judiciously in my interactions with law enforcement. I respected and revered our military who were charged with protecting the public.

Len and the boys had much for which to forgive me. To be fair, Len and I began our own policy of forgiveness. Every time Seth secured free tickets for us to a Sea World or Mystic Aquarium where he had secured an internship, we deducted the cost of the tickets from the cost of his veterinary school education. Subsequent subtractions accompanied each complimentary admission to another aquarium in another city from Charleston to San Diego to Gatlinburg. Given the joy he brought to our lives, he has long since paid us back in full. The ongoing joke joined other anecdotes in our family folklore.

Providing graduate level education for both sons was our pleasure and our responsibility. They excelled academically while we managed to remain free of debtors' prison.

One weekend we met two sets of best friends from college for a weekend in Mystic during Seth's internship. We enjoyed the antics of the sea mammals and the backstage tours of the tanks. We saw elaborate operations most tourists never see. We dined at a local casino during which alarms went off and everyone evacuated. Someone sprayed Mace while we stood on a very long line to the buffet. As people broke from the queue to hasten outside, our doctor and lawyer friends advised us to remain where we were, enabling us to proceed to the front of the line. We were already seated and digging in when the emergency ended and hungry evacuees returned to line up. That night, Len turned up the volume on the car radio so the six of us could dance to oldies in the parking lot.

On another weekend, cousins arrived to enjoy a complimentary tour of the Mystic Aquarium with their twin sons. It was July 4th weekend, highlighted by the young twin's fascination with the tiny seahorses and enormous walruses. Lying back on blankets in a grassy park, we oohed and aahed at fireworks slamming into the night sky. On a visit to the northwest to see our younger son, he took us to dinner at a lavish buffet and then led us to a bridge overlooking valleys below. Elaborate fireworks displays appeared over each of the valleys as patterns of colored lights sped into higher reaches of sky, only to dissolve and disappear over the mountainous patchwork of rural communities.

Len had "that talk" with our sons about compliance with police. When driving, it is obligatory to follow police directives. That talk was supposedly reserved to black Americans. Learning to be deferential to authority, especially armed law enforcement, seems essential for all young men. In rapid succession, Len modeled that compliance in several unexpected encounters.

Not long after the Tucson tumult, Len had another couple of "brushes" with the law. Back in NJ, he took a lunchtime stroll through a park outside his place of employment. Law enforcement approached to ask what he was doing. He explained. They were pursuing a "bad guy." Len was not that guy. Case closed.

At about the same time, police cars and vans with sirens blaring and lights flashing pulled over his van. Upon seeing Len up close, one radioed the others, "It's a white guy." He explained that they were pursuing suspects in a van that matched his van in appearance. It was not racial profiling but a description that made his van suspect, though not its driver. Another case closed. Len was not targeted because of harassment or profiling. He respectfully followed directions. The cops did their dangerous job when they stopped him and let him go. That's life. Sometimes that's death. I learned about these incidents after the fact and did not exacerbate them.

In college, Len volunteered to work with a civil rights group focused on improving education for minorities in New Brunswick. "Education in Action" enlisted his efforts. We both participated in civil rights marches. Len joined a couple of civil rights organizations and was active in the integrated middle school community in which he taught.

Len completed a master's degree while teaching and went on to lead the local NEA as President. He refused to defend the indefensible behavior of some entitled teachers who counted on the union to protect jobs and pay increments they did not necessarily deserve. He would not fight for a teacher guilty of chronic lateness. He did negotiate with the Board to win the biggest starting salary, $8,000 per year, in the nation.

His advocacy cost him a sabbatical, a much-anticipated trip to East Africa that the Board denied him. They punished his effectiveness as negotiator. Reprisals notwithstanding, he went on to become a team leader introducing interdisciplinary studies and providing scientific hands-on experiments for his students. He excelled as a teacher.

His students constructed and launched rockets. They incubated chicken eggs which Len brought home to our apartment during Christmas vacation. Upon hatching, the alpha chicken he named "Diablo" bonded with Len. Diablo followed him around the apartment like a dog taught to heel. It rode on Len's shoulder. Diablo substituted for a dog with feathers.

Len worked summers at a Title I Science and Reading Summer Camp. Eventually he ran it.

Groups of middle school students spent several weeks at a conference facility in NY State. They benefitted from classes in the mornings and traditional camp activities in the afternoons and evenings. They enjoyed sports, swimming, fishing and fish fries, and barbecues. They took hikes along forested trails and attended late-night astronomical seminars. They dissected frogs and danced to Jackson 5 hits in the conference hall. They discovered that learning is fun..

Len assisted with their acculturation by instituting simple behavioral standards. He instructed them to take one chop or piece of chicken at a time from a passing platter. There were eight chops for eight people seated at a table. He assured them that seconds were available. He taught them that etiquette demanded you take one at a time. Some students from large families, unaccustomed to having enough, found all this quite new. Len offered a remedial course in table manners, group living, and extended family dynamics in a bucolic setting. Secure in the knowledge that second and third helpings appeared if requested, they took one helping at a time. Progress!

Len took advantage of his camp jobs to indulge his interest in photography. His initial focus on bees busy with flowers and other scenes of nature shifted to videos. Soon he documented the activities of the campers and counselors, who were his fellow teachers. He also displayed his first interest in theater.

One night he orchestrated a reading of Poe's "The Telltale Heart." He placed a blanket-covered coffin on a darkened stage. He sat me alongside the coffin to read the scary story by candlelight. Len rigged a clothesline contraption from off stage to the coffin/chest. At the appropriate moment I sprang from my seat, shouting that I had no way to stop the beating of that horrible heart. At the same time a ghostlike shroud-wrapped "figure" traveled the clothesline to the stage. The coffin lid opened and out jumped one of the campers.

It did not help that a huge storm hit that night with growling thunder and scorching lightning bolts hurtling all around. The terrified kids in the audience fled shrieking into the night. The scripted tumult performed in Poe's tale persuaded the campers that I was a witch. It took some days of working with them on a camp newsletter and reassurances that I was not a malevolent force to overcome that impression.

Over the years, Len's interest in photography and theater grew. I can still see him in the unfinished portion of our basement developing his photos in a makeshift darkroom. He filled albums and covered the walls of three houses with scenes of nature and family celebrations. He created galleries with head shots and candid photos from rehearsals for community theaters and private repertory groups. He lovingly removed some evidence of aging from aging ingenues. He performed plastic surgery and administered Botox with photo-shopped touch ups of me in photographs. I shall be eternally grateful.

He also progressed in his educational career. After teaching for years in NYC and New Jersey, he earned recommendations for a new job as an educational planner by administrators appreciative of his professionalism and cognizant of his potential. In that capacity, he worked with superintendents, principals, teachers, parents, and federal and state education officials and colleges.

He devoted himself to guaranteeing the legislative promise of a "thorough and efficient education" for NJ students. Always professionally reliable in completing his tasks prior to deadlines, he came to the attention of other superintendents whose planners were less punctual. They called on him to troubleshoot. He assisted other county superintendents whose planners were not as efficient or professional as Len. He was equally ahead of schedule in his personal life.

At any time, he might have several suitcases packed months in advance for future trips. I emulated his punctuality in performance of my professional duties. I customarily prepared for evaluations, conferences, grant writing assignments, workshops, and other projects days to weeks before they were due. The same habits carried over into theater. I memorized my script and blocking for roles prior to the first rehearsal, if possible. Len prepared head shots, posters, and boards of candid photos weeks or months before each show. Deadlines did not carry death sentences for failure to meet them but were taken seriously.

He won the respect of the people with whom he worked. He cut through the labyrinth of bureaucratic laws and regulations. He developed gifted and talented programs offering college courses to deserving high school students. He made sure lab facilities met safety standards, and that accessibility was provided. He helped local administrators and teachers uphold testing protocols. Educational standards were paramount. When I became an Assistant Principal, I emulated Len's conduct as an administrator.

When the time to retire arrived, someone warned him of boredom and an early death if he retired too soon. What would he do with his time? His previous boss wanted him to return to NJ to do consulting work. But he was done with that stage of his life and ready to embark on new adventures. Len planned to be too busy to be bored.

Len eagerly embraced new challenges, whether to hike a new trail, try a new recipe (which he always doctored to individual taste), or sample an unfamiliar culture. On our first trip to France, Len packed with confidence. We would make our way given his high school introduction to the language. We felt equipped to engage in conversation or ask directions, fortified by our friend Lee's major and my minor in the subject. None of us counted on the indifference of some French purists to our efforts to communicate. They damned us for failures in accent authenticity.

One day we ventured into a delicatessen in Paris, trying to purchase two ham and cheese baguettes for a picnic in the Tuileries. The sandwich commandant refused to combine ham and cheese on a single baguette. He insisted we select one ingredient or the other. We tried to counter his spartan stubbornness with an offer to purchase two baguettes. We would combine the ham and cheese on one baguette, and he could either keep or discard the other one. Non, non, and non!

Hunger dictated compliance. Finally, we obeyed his rules. We bought separate single-ingredient sandwiches, which we then combined on a vacant park bench. We deposited the extra bread where birds could enjoy it. While reviewing that escapade, we watched a hygiene-compromised man wander over to a fountain where he proceeded to wash his feet and private parts. Not all the sights of Paris mirrored those of Versailles! But even that appalling vision failed to diminish our appetites.

Coincidentally, the day before Len earned the nickname "Monsieur Grand Pied." Our hotel offered a public bathroom on each floor. Outfitted with a small bar of soap and a scratchy, no-longer absorbent towel, Len ventured into the dirty shower to perform his ablutions. Having dropped the soap, he refused to retrieve it from the disgusting floor. The filth of centuries appeared to have coated the floors, walls, and ceilings of the pension. Paris afforded historic grime for $5 a day. It was all our budgets could accommodate. While the rest of us came equipped with shower shoes, he did not have any. We tried to remedy that with a visit to a shoe store.

Two women working in the shop took turns measuring his feet, sized 12 or 13 at the time. They alternated climbing a ladder to retrieve boxes of shoes that were more like plastic sandals than shower shoes. They took down only one box at a time. As they removed the sandals, they remarked each time that the shoes were too small, and his feet were too big. I do not remember if Len made a purchase, but he was Monsieur Grand Pied for the rest of the trip and sometimes, to this day. That was only one of many nicknames I inflicted on Len. The rest remain secret for the sake of our marriage.

Moving West, I suffered a panic attack when we crossed the Mississippi River. It suggested an exorcism removing all traces of the East. After all, we were leaving everyone and everything we knew, from best friends to the dentist. We left the land of the familiar. We bade farewell to the local dry cleaner and cinema, the Chinese takeout restaurant and the roads we drove commuting to work. We journeyed a thousand miles from daily routines that started at 5:30 AM every morning for thirty years to a new, alarm-clock free life.

Our destined Arizona awaited us, still more than another thousand miles away. We moved to a discomforting if beautiful place. It could be as menacing as the sounds of packs of coyotes hunting for jack rabbits in the undeveloped desert behind our new home. Arizona beauty was bizarre, and the wilderness was weird. I was unnerved.

I left a house I had lived in for twenty-seven years, in which I had raised my sons. I shut down a thirty-year career I had loved. In the months before my retirement, my eyes closed when I stopped the car at red lights. One day, my vision blurred as I crossed the block to the house. I could not measure the depth of the step from the curb to the street. A visit to a neurologist confirmed that I worked too hard and had to stop.

My sister and Len pressured me to stop working. Len, with as much solemnity as he could muster, threatened to move West with or without me, pointing out that I was jeopardizing my health by refusing to retire. All the extra hours I had put in amounted to another decade of service. I was not ready to quit, but I was exhausted. My body quit. Finally, I acquiesced to age and prepared for the next stage in life.

That final crossing of the Rubicon in St. Louis made it impossible to avoid the truth. My old life was over. A new life awaited beyond the arch-framed city. Len would see me through to give me that paradise. He delivered the life in the great outdoors I had always relished on family vacations. I put aside my fear of the unknown and embraced Len's dream, making it my own.

No realistic danger ever existed that Len would die of boredom. He embraced the West with the enthusiasm he mustered for both old hobbies and new interests. He played out his childhood dream of being a cowboy. He donned dusters and cowboy boots, inlaid turquoise rings and bandanas. He stacked up Stetsons and leather belts with silver buckles.

He ventured repeatedly into Tombstone, site of the Earps' historic showdown. He read many exposes, all claiming to tell the true story of their legendary saga. We ate in restaurants built atop mineshafts. The owner of Big Nose Kate's Saloon introduced himself to Len and some friends. We were a foursome he figured might have come from his hometown, NYC. Cowboy boots did nothing to disguise New York accents. We returned frequently to our new friend's restaurant where a warm welcome was assured, and a discounted bill accompanied the usual fare.

Watching the Hollywood spectaculars, *Tombstone* and *Wyatt Earp*, set the stage for our fifteen years of combing deserts and mountains. We haunted mining towns like Bisbee and Jerome and Wild West scenarios like Sonoita. Len became hooked on the West. I shared his addiction.

Obsessed with both movies featuring epic sweeps of our new "backyard," we watched them repeatedly. Kevin Costner and Kurt Russell offered splendid versions of Wyatt Earp. Dressed in typical western gear, Len surprised a boy touring Old Tucson Studio with his mom. They ventured inside a replica of an old train station with a ticket agent stationed up front. Suddenly the boy called out, "Mom, this guy moved!" It was Len.

Frequently mistaken for one of the actors reprising the shootout at the O.K. Corral, my husband delighted in playing the part when we visited Tombstone. All of Arizona, if not the world, transformed itself into a stage. Thoroughly occupied, Len, my leading man, avoided boredom.

We loved that town with boardwalks over dusty, often rain-flooded streets and bullet-pierced saloons.

We explored Boot Hill for an incredible snapshot in time. A black man born into slavery lived one hundred years, witnessing abolition and the dropping of the atomic bomb before he died. Boot Hill preserved a time of segregated burial sites for whites, Chinese, and blacks. Jews were buried in another site maintained by Indians and Jews.

Today, tourists of all backgrounds track the headstones of the bullet-ridden corpses of the notorious cowboys at that historic cemetery. They dine in restaurants decorated with bars and posters of the 1880s. It belongs to all of us now. It traces the history of a self-correcting territory and republic. Like Len's students at the summer camp, we had fun learning.

A town once notorious for the high life and sudden death of high rollers hosted celebrity gamblers. Journalist William Randolph Hearst journeyed to The Bird Cage Theater for all-night, big-stakes poker games. Prostitution employed more women than teaching positions. The Chinese community dispensed opium. Ranchers, miners, shopkeepers, judges, newspaper publishers, bartenders, undertakers, and everyday folk lived side by side with cattle rustlers, killers, and corrupt politicians.

Some things never seem to change until they do. Tombstone continues to attract tourists, but an earthquake re-routed the San Pedro River, destroying its status as the fastest-growing town east of San Francisco. It flooded the mines and ended the silver rush. Tourism replaced silver mining. The town changed. The legend survived.

We alternated climbing different mountain ranges that surrounded our valley. We hiked on rocks as multi-hued as the sea. We passed quarries of decorative stones and gleaming splinters of quartz. We followed blazed trails leading us from saguaro at the foot to alpine groves at the top.

Altitude provided a range of habitats from the desert mesquite to the evergreens, firs, and pines just below the tundra. Temperatures cooled as altitude provided respite from summer heat.

We hiked as a pair and accompanied family and friends who visited us to our majestic mountains. We drove my beloved Aunt Ann to five parallel waterfalls on one mountain slope. Hiking another, she remarked in delight that all the stones on the trail were colored pinks, salmons, and turquoise hues. That sort of shared discovery made our new home magical. Len's eagerness to share our discoveries led our many guests to rebook.

Len befriended a key performer at Old Tucson Studios. He would nod to her when we visited with family and friends. Adorned in prostitute chic finery of the period, she returned a wink. She would give them her special attention.

Stuntmen performed feats right out of the movies. They shot each other from buildings, fell onto hay-covered wagons, and enacted melodramas to thrill our grandchildren. Rides in stagecoaches and panning for gold nuggets, or fool's gold, made visits memorable. I still did a little consulting work, but employment faded from my rear-view mirror as Len mapped new outdoor adventures in our Arizona frontier.

Len discovered the steam engine powered train that rode across the pronghorn friendly plains from Williams, Arizona. The train offered an unimpeded view of the San Francisco Peaks of Flagstaff as it chugged to the south rim of the Grand Canyon. Perched on Rte. 66, Williams opened the time machine to another day, with old-fashioned malt shops and classic cars. Shops and western-style restaurants featured blue grass singers. Windows displayed hypnotizing geodes, Indian jewelry, and lots of western wear. Len, dressed for the occasion in cowboy gear, fit right in.

We enjoyed a show during the train ride in comfortable coaches lit by large windows and the adornments of a bygone age in travel. Actors posing as train robbers galloped alongside boarded, pulled guns, and robbed the customers. Our forewarned younger granddaughter refused to hand over her possessions. She put on her own mask, Len's bandanna, and offered a portrait in Annie Oakley style resistance. She performed the role of a bank robber, threatening to divest the professional actors of their loot. Our granddaughter Ellen made a splendid curly blonde bandit. Banjo players and country and western singers also entertained in the theater on train tracks.

At the canyon, the bus made several stops, allowing passengers to walk along short segments of the rim trail to experience the air and scenery of the national park. California condors, restored to the park, swept from their rocky perches to other locales. The winds were strong, whispering Indian secrets in the shadows. As the pine-perfumed day progressed and the light changed, Len grabbed his camera to catch the changing colors of the canyon walls. The winding vein of the blue Colorado River shimmered below. The canyon caught fire as the sun kept to its schedule. The views mesmerized our family and friends on the three excursions Len booked for us.

We had a routine of sorts, living in a resort retirement community with frequent visits back East to see family. We welcomed a continuous pattern of visits from friends and family to participate in our paradise. We took a brisk five-mile walk each day. Despite being a pathetic athlete, I indulged myself in every moment I could spend outdoors.

While still working, I took the dog on half-hour jaunts through dark evenings of inclement NJ weather. On holidays and weekends, I imposed forced marches on an occasionally reluctant beagle. Len and I took twenty-mile bike rides to a diner for breakfast in New York state on weekends while we still lived in North Jersey. We worked off breakfasts at diners by circling trails in county parks with friends. Decades of routine paled beside our retirement in Arizona with a bright sun beckoning us to indulge in daily outdoor activities. Landlocked, we missed the sea. Frequent trips to the West Coast or back East fed that longing. Meanwhile, we had the desert and mountains.

16

WESTERN SKIES

In Arizona, we continued to ride bicycles until Len witnessed a horrible accident. A car struck a properly outfitted bicyclist just blocks from our home and yards away. Len dialed 911 while the man bled out. We sold our bicycles, but not before we had driven our sons up to Madera Canyon. At Madera, the three of them would mount bicycles transported in the van to coast downhill and then pedal furiously for miles back to our home. We loved biking. But after the accident, our two-wheelers followed us into retirement.

We swam almost all year. I struggled through my customary single lap followed by a brief rest. I repeated the exercise, lap by torturous lap, until I completed a half mile. Len, a fish by nature, swam one or two miles a day, using flippers and a mask. His long-synchronized stroke registered as effortlessly as that of any sea creature.

For some years, when we visited La Jolla with our kids, he swam out past a buoy a half mile offshore. He ventured past the shelf where the floor dropped off, the water temperature chilled and the currents provided resistance. Finally, a couple of documented great white shark attacks persuaded him to stay closer to shore and confine most of his swimming to pools.

We broke our relaxed schedule so frequently that it never took on the disadvantages of a rigid routine. We migrated to the Pacific as often as some birds. We hiked Torrey Pines and watched seals at La Jolla Cove. When my sister and her husband joined us on trips, she identified the succulents, cacti, and wildflowers lining the trails. We waited for Len to get just the right camera shot of a tidepool teeming with crabs or a flowering bush humming with insects.

California prospered, teeming with tourists and newly arrived residents. We savored snapshots of wonderful trips when proximity and the pull of the Pacific occasioned weeks away from Arizona. We moved when the lure of the Southwest succumbed to dystopian developments. We have not visited since. Places like Yosemite and La Jolla remain in my heart. They continue to beckon, along with Greer and Mount Lemmon in Arizona. But they are no longer what they were.

We had fifteen years of resort living in the West in a home we envisioned as our forever home. I could not have hoped for more. Changes in our health and changes in those communities validated our decision. It was time to leave. The next stage in our life awaited back on the East Coast. There would be no forever home. We simply relocated with our forever love.

We introduced our grandson to San Diego's Old Town on one of his visits to Delmar with our son Seth and my sister and her husband. He went through an art museum only to reconstruct his path, showing his favorite seascapes to his Great Uncle Jason. Marc was a little kid, already alert to the wonders of painting. It became an interest he shared with his grandfather, attending art auctions, making a few sanctioned "purchases" as gifts, and perusing art books. Marc's great aunt, my sister, intrigued him with her paintings. He especially liked the sculptures of antiquity but later developed a taste for some modern painters as well as the old masters.

Marc learned early to hike some distances in the Cascades, the Rockies, the Smokies, and the streets around our Arizona home. He pointed out all the strange cacti as he walked with his sisters and me. He noted that it was a bad idea to touch anything that grew there. Our dog, slower to learn that lesson, stepped too close to the thorny needles. I often extracted jumping cholla needles that embedded themselves in his tender feet.

Len introduced me to the sky. That sounds strange. But what you see in the anemic, smog-blurred, and electric light-dulled skies of eastern cities is not what the West offers. Montana deserves the label, "Big Sky Country." On our first trip out West, Len rented mounts upon arrival. With one boot in a stirrup, Len swung over his saddle horse and rode out into the endless blue horizon.

Unfortunately, I could not control my horse. He decided it was quitting time, turned around, and headed back to the stable. A surprised hand offered me another mount, Danny Boy. He had the energy of a horse just exhumed. We set off again, Len riding slightly ahead, eager to gallop into the sun. I called out to say that my horse had stopped to graze.

"Kick it," Len advised. Despite wearing soft sandals incapable of hurting the disobedient horse, I demurred. The horse ignored me. He knew who had control. Disappointed and no doubt, somewhat ashamed, Len turned his horse around to follow me into the corral.

The cowboy was probably born bareback, riding a horse down the birth canal to the wide-open spaces of Montana. Before he could venture a comment or offer another horse, Len paid the wrangler, got back into the car, and continued West. I was still his passenger for life. That is love.

Montana skies were breathtakingly clear. We marveled at both day and nighttime vistas. We would see magnificent skies in the Sierras where each pull out on the switchback offered an entirely different swath of stars.

But Arizona skies delivered the most impressive scenes. The clear winner in the competition of celestial constellations, each expanse of southwestern sky reaffirmed our decision to retire there. From our southern Arizona hub, we traveled widely throughout the west, pursuing our dreams, always grateful for the skies.

We visited Arizona's Kitts Peak, an observatory operated by a university consortium. We looked through telescopes to spot distant planets and stars. We used the naked eye to view constellations so vast they claimed supremacy over the imagination. Some nights we stood outside our garage and watched one light after another blink on. Displays of crystal chandeliers illuminated the darkening ceiling above. Midnight skies became velvet-lined jewel boxes and display cases against which diamond stars sparkled.

During the monsoon season, bolts of lightning heralded the apocalypse. Lightning strikes lit up the space between clouds, between clouds and the ground, and between the sky and the mountain tops. Percussive thunder more nightmarish than martial enveloped our house and our street. Mystery encompassed us against rumbles in the dimming skies and crashes in the dark.

Deafening cymbals, streaking light, and torrents of horizontal and vertical water returned us to archetypal memories of what thunderstorms must have been like for our ancestors. All the progress from astrology to astronomy could not stamp the skies with the assurances of science when imagination took control. The breathtaking storms rivaled Independence Day fireworks displays. Life out West captivated us. Boredom never conquered us.

Towns and unincorporated village officials strictly regulated streetlights to maintain the visibility required for astronomical observations. To venture out at night assumed risk. Snakes spread out over the still warm macadam, and Len taught me to look down as well as up. We encountered rattlers in Saguaro National Park and in Sequoia. Snake skinned boots and belts paraded the destiny of some ill-fated members of the deadly species.

Eagles clutched high branches in Yellowstone. Other eagles flew, talons up front, before our boat in Alaska. They skirmished for fish with droplets of Bering Sea cold dripping from their wings. Wherever I looked, beauty appeared. When I looked up, there was Len, ready to guide me, rescue me, and love me.

It seemed that every week Len planned another adventure for us. He reserved a B & B in Julian. We arrived at the picturesque, small tourist town ensconced above a lake in pine-forested terrain. A few hours east of San Diego, Julian prized a main street festooned with trinkets of a bygone America. Antique shops held an array of items long since thrown out and forgotten by American consumers. Items included kitchen gadgets, operated manually, but so vastly superior to the more primitive methods that preceded them.

The Julian Cider Mill opened a full-scale jam, preserve, and jelly operation to interested tourists. They operated an assembly line producing fruit ciders with samples at the end. They made the ciders and preserves from the fruit orchards that dotted the countryside. We ordered them for years while we lived in Arizona and even ventured to pay for exorbitant shipping when we relocated to an address on the East Coast.

Locals who did not work in the busy, booth-lined restaurants and bakeries, relaxed on porches. They sipped coffee, consumed small talk, and shared community. Most shops offered fruit pies. It was obligatory to go from one bakery to another restaurant, sampling different flavored pies. Combinations of berries that created delicious moments of sheer joy competed for our favorites. Ordering pie a la mode felt mandatory.

Pie places are very big out West. We remember favorites atop Mt. Lemmon in Tucson and at the base of Mineral King outside Sequoia National Park. A special orchard sandwiched between Sequoia and Kings Canyon afforded more nutritious snacks. We stopped on several occasions to stock up on varieties of apples. We tore into our supply on day one and nibbled assiduously on days two and three. We devoured apples until nothing remained in the crate but a few stems and leaves, and a core one of us mistakenly deposited.

On one return trip from California to Arizona, Len took a new route through an untraveled desert. No rest stops. No gas stations. No fast-food facilities. No traffic. We traveled like ghosts across the miles, mesmerized by the unearthly landscape and menaced by the emptiness. Death Valley offered similar scenery, filled by harsh, looming rocks with shadows lurking everywhere. A detour promised adventure and always delivered.

Len drove us east to an area of Arizona known as a pit stop on the path of migrating sandhill cranes. They sequestered the sky, their huge wings opening like the ghastly robes of Nosferatu. They landed by the thousands in farmers' fields. While they searched for the last bits of the harvested crop, thousands more flew in to join them. We watched amazed for some time as one squadron after another landed. Len took photos until the fields were entirely covered. It was another adventure to make friends with the migratory sandhill cranes.

Len discovered a rustic B & B in the White Mountains of Greer. We visited the Painted Desert and Petrified Forest along with a pottery place in Zuni land. After a couple of days of hiking in the forests and headwaters of the Little

Colorado River, we drove past flocks of wild turkeys and remote log cabins. We wound through the quarries that provided ore and decorative rock to residents of retirement communities like ours. We skirted an old mining town but did not learn its story until years later.

An entire small class centered on its football team signed up to fight in Vietnam. They all died. The children comprised the most precious commodity in that community. Our older son enlisted for the War on Terror. We were fortunate. His patriotism taught us how precious he was. He survived. They all became our sons as our capacity for gratitude to our warriors grew. Decorative rocks, Gold Star families, the grandeur of the South Rim, and monsoon storms taught us to love our Arizona home.

Once Len led a couple of dear friends who were visiting us to the Buenos Aires Wildlife Refuge. Situated south of our home, it lay closer to the border. It unveiled an area of low elevation. Nearby mountain ranges typified most of Arizona. Lions, Jackals, and pronghorns once frequented this area. Boardwalks made the area accessible. Trails stitched wetlands to solid ground. A giant cottonwood spread its huge umbrella over the space where deer and other animals still wandered. Taking in the scenery, our college buddies Sam and Daphne asked if we would let them know next time we visited Bryce.

They had traveled the world, from Nepal to Scandinavia, but never got to Bryce. Len, always the consummate host, offered to book us a few days at Bryce if they were willing to shorten our stay at the refuge. They agreed and we were soon on our way.

On this visit to Bryce, unlike a former one with our sons, the colors contrasted even more vividly. Banks of sun-bleached snow highlighted the vibrant green of the trees that lined the trails. The celestial blue of the heavens contrasted with the burnt red of the rocks for which Bryce is famous. The strange formations, hoodoos, stood like chess pieces on a board big enough for the gods to play on. We found it all achingly beautiful, and we hiked.

As the trail narrowed, the piles of snow glistened with the surface melt released by the midday sun. Our progress slowed. A single slip could send one of us tumbling down a steep, rocky slope dotted with trees. We moved to less perilous trails. Knowing your limits emerged as one of life's lessons in humility. Len always cautioned that it was time to return when the least able hiker started to tire. He usually insisted on heading back before that happened. He got us into unbelievable places, and I always believed he would always get us out.

Another time we met our "Bryce" friends in Yosemite. Len rented a house and arrived early to purchase groceries before heading to Fresno Airport to pick them up. They arrived late due to unanticipated work issues that delayed them. They had additional days of their vacation left to spend after the Yosemite segment ended. The rental expired after a few days of guiding them to Yosemite highlights. Len introduced them to giant Sequoias and the valley crossed by the Merced River. He led them to Bridal Falls veiling the granite in the mist and a rainbow arc. He mapped a climb up Lembert Dome near glacial Lake Tenaya.

Len, our stalwart guide, rose each morning to prepare a hot breakfast and pack a lunch for the four of us. I acted as his sous chef. He attended to every detail. With a few extra days of vacation, he reserved a rustic motel on the outskirts of the White Mountains in California. I had read about the bristlecone pines; a rare species found in only a few places on the planet. We always wanted to see them. This was our chance. They predate modern times. They predate the reign of the pharaohs. We seized the time to be still and listen to the wind. We sensed all the great transformations since they first took root. It was a time to feel insignificant and blessed, simultaneously.

This pair of beloved college friends first introduced us to the West when they invited us to La Jolla. Len happily facilitated their first trip to Bryce. We took many trips together. I had the good fortune to become part of a sextet consisting of our college alumni. The two couples of our best friends were intelligent, articulate, curious, and adventurous. Sam and Daphne, Lee and Hailey completed our sextet. And as our sons pointed out, they were the only people they knew of all our friends and acquaintances who would travel well with us...or travel with us at all.

17

WILDLIFE

In Arizona, nature put on a show. We watched meteor showers from our own front yard. Neighbors who trespassed over our decorative rock and cactus plants included quail. The mother started out with perhaps twenty knuckle-sized babies. Her offspring dwindled down just a few weeks later as road runners, coyotes, and heedless drivers decimated their numbers. Predation also culled the jackrabbits from our area. But Javelina, sharp-toothed and irascible, walked boldly across our property. Another interloper, a big horned owl, settled down with no risk of being disturbed at dusk.

Assertive bobcats felt entitled to stalk our premises. Once, Len escorted a neighbor walking a small dog a block from our home to her house. He sent me home and instructed her to pick up her appetizing little dog and stay close to him. He relied on his height to protect them from an attack. After he escorted her and her dog to her home, he returned to ours. The bobcat flicked his tail and walked off. Predators tend to be arrogant.

Coyotes proved ubiquitous, like hummingbirds. Roadrunners, such affable animated creatures, turned out to be serious predators. We witnessed their meals in flight as they snapped up butterflies. The hummingbirds hovered like helicopters above flowering bushes. The hunted focused on the nectar in our plants and failed to heed the approaching danger. The yellow butterflies paid the price of turning cartwheels of disinterest, only to end up in the unrelenting beaks of the roadrunners. Our animal neighbors grabbed dinner from our front yard foliage while we grilled beneath the backyard ramada.

We encountered a huge snake in the garage, along with scorpions and spiders. When we traveled, a neighbor snapped the photo of a mountain lion who left paw prints on the rocks in our backyard. We spotted deer strolling nonchalantly downtown and two pairs of golden eagles riding the thermals outside Elephant Head. Welcome to Arizona, where you need never be bored.

It is true that the tulips did not bloom during our spring visit on a river cruise to Holland, but Len showed me fields of poppies carpeting the mountains outside a town closer to the border in location and closer to the old west in culture.

He chaperoned and chauffeured me through a different type of wildlife when I worked for the census. I conducted head counts of people who did not want to be found or counted. One former law enforcement officer, who worked for the census, got assigned to that remote haven for "independent" spirits. He showed up at the ranch of a shotgun-toting character who threatened him. The character had chosen to live off the official grid.

The census worker, a former officer, quit the ranch immediately. He quit the job.

I did not find urban danger daunting. I had situational awareness in New York City. As a non-resident welfare case worker, I knocked on doors in housing projects and slum apartments. But rural danger took me unawares. Threats were unfamiliar. It was not my home turf.

Local census officials tapped me with a dangerous caseload spread over remote areas. It assigned me to the surroundings for trailer parks and dumps. Another place left me with foreboding. The place seemed located as far away from Tucson as possible for any place to be within the United States. Residents barricaded their "community" with barbed wire and pit bulls.

Len would not let me get out of the car. He insisted on driving me to every address. After looking around and conducting a danger assessment, he backed up or turned around on a few occasions to drive on to the next neighborhood on the caseload.

The government required three phone calls per person, followed by three home visits per person. That concluded the obligation to count that individual.

My husband saved my life by establishing his own conscientious but survival-strong instinct to complete the requirement short of the three visits. For impossible-to-locate people or outwardly dangerous sites, Len had me furnish a paper explanation. No one else, certifiably crazy, volunteered to conduct a follow-up visit. Some regulations and tasks are insane. Fortunately for me, Len was saner than I. He knew when to say "no."

18

WARNINGS AND HISTORY

Len's hunger to learn about the West never abated but had to make room for his growing interest in WWII. Books about D-Day, the Pacific campaigns, and the great Allied generals lined up along books about the Earps, Doc Holliday, and Arizona's path from territory to statehood. He credited that war and the Americans who fought it with having given us our lives. Born in 1942 and 1943 respectively, we would not have survived an Axis victory. Len started reading histories and novels. One day, he remarked that members of our Temple included some WWII veterans. They were aging.

Len determined to register the veteran contributions to an oral history he elicited and published. Len and I initiated a joint project to profile WWII veterans for our monthly Temple newsletter. The opening profiles were well received, concluding with the telling of thirteen tales.

My husband established a template with a questionnaire. I served as secretary. We furnished lunch for the veteran and spouse or significant other of his or her choice. We stationed a box of tissues at the ready. After lunch with small talk on the side, we began the interview in earnest. Len reassured the veterans that he would not print anything without their approval. They had final control as editors.

Several confided that they had never spoken of their war experiences before, to anyone. Some expressed guilt for having survived. Others rejected any suggestion that they had done anything noteworthy or heroic. The real heroes, they maintained, gave their lives and never came home. As we listened, we followed up with additional questions, where appropriate. There were tears all around. Within a couple of weeks of each interview, Len and I prepared the profile.

Len verified details such as dates, battlefields, and other specifics to ensure that memory was not adversely affected by age. As the newsletters appeared, interest in the project intensified. Only one veteran declined to tell his story. We respected his privacy but regretted that his story would die with him. He witnessed a history we were determined to preserve. The stories proved singularly distinct.

In our sampler of heroism, the selflessness of our veterans shone. They spent their youth in the vanguard of patriots who saved America, the West, and Len and me.

One of the veterans served as a flight surgeon in the Pacific. His generous provisions of medicines to Catholic nuns treating lepers led them to conclude he must be a Catholic. When he explained that he was not Catholic or even a Christian, they were stunned. When he told them he was a Jew, they were surprised. They also expressed how grateful they were.

The military tasked one veteran, a band leader, with raising morale. He never forgave himself for having secured positions of safety for himself and his orchestra. That left others to take their places on the battlefield. One infantry man dealt with logistics for our troops fighting in Europe. A woman worked as a secretary on the Manhattan Project without ever knowing what it was all about.

The local newspaper editor learned about the project. She embarked on a third edition to come out weekly every Sunday. She kickstarted that expansion with the publication of one profile each week. Len summoned a meeting of the veterans to reassure them that he would not proceed without their permission. They agreed. The Sunday addition succeeded. It boosted sales, subscriptions, and interest in the veterans who made up a substantial portion of our retirement community. Fans snapped up every episode in every new edition.

Before she published the final profile, the editor met with us to insist that we receive payment for our work. Len refused. He committed himself to serving the veterans and resolved to do nothing self-serving. He suggested that she donate the funds to the Temple to finance a dinner for the membership to honor the veterans for their sacrifice.

The veterans felt delighted when Len consulted with them. The dinner featured speakers and entertainment. A U.S. Senator responded with a citation acknowledging their contributions. The project was therapeutic. The veterans seemed somehow assuaged of some of their nightmares and tribulations. They enjoyed the camaraderie as they learned more about each other than they usually gleaned at bagel and lox Sunday brunches. The newspaper editor appeared on the dais as a valued guest of honor. She, in turn, honored the veterans.

Sermons and readings for the High Holy Days, Holocaust Remembrance programs, and sporadic services took on heightened meaning. Len and I felt an irrepressible joy that comes from elevating people who deserve it. We knew we owed everything to these people. We wrote a follow up letter to the editor in which we offered to share our template with members of other faiths and interest groups who might want to replicate the project with their own veterans. We had no takers. We appreciated the heritage of all those heroes whose stories too often died with them. Our lives are their legacy.

Len worked as my researcher and co-presenter in our public speaking engagements. He also gave presentations ranging from the carnage of WWII to the terrorism unleashed by jihadists. Len offered our audiences a break from my higher decibel level and higher octave delivery.

The willfully blind among our contacts preferred personal estrangement to the classical liberal approach of dialogue and well-tolerated dissent.

Len's fortitude helped me fend off the paralysis of fear, as telephoned threats tried to shut down presentations. We marched into the thick of the fray, just like we did during the civil rights movement.

Len left his mark on the community. He organized a chapter of the neighborhood watch to protect yearlong and snowbird residents. We also organized opposition to the builder's falsehoods about the number and length of nails used to secure roof shingles. Each summer monsoon, swaths of shingles were blown off to be replaced and repaired at the homeowner's expense. Our community protest resulted in a judge's decision to halt all building of new homes until such time as the roofs had been repaired at the builder's expense.

Scheduled to present a talk on Islamism I was threatened. Halfway through my presentation, a man wearing a jihadist headdress interrupted. "We're here and more of us are coming." I told him I would not tolerate interference and reminded him he would have an opportunity to raise his objections when I finished. When Len stood, he sat. I completed my talk. No violence occurred. The promised Q & A happened.

Len sent out warnings about the threat of a porous border to ranchers and hikers. He issued alerts about the politicization of academia.

We felt betrayed by teacher unions that abandoned the pupils they were hired by taxpayers to serve. The NEA bore no resemblance to the professional organization Len headed years before. Len and I took the same route from earnest union members and leaders to opponents of public employee unions.

Calculate another win for anti-American and anti-Western values. As literacy and numeracy standards fell, costs rose. We worried about the academic deficits lowering prospects for our grandchildren's future.

Len had fought for scholarship, civics and civility. He paid for his fidelity to empiricism and faith. Undaunted by intimidation, he continued to do his homework. We both continue to champion discourse, dialogue, and free speech.

Len still sends out information, hoping to pierce the bubble. I offer our analysis on podcasts, talk shows, and Substack posts. Len cheers me on.

Scheduled as the opening act for two experts on jihadism, I was disappointed when the threat level rose and the casino owners caved. They surrendered to pressure. They canceled the event, unwilling to risk an attack or to invest in the security necessary to preserve freedom of speech. Len lamented yet another capitulation to intimidation. I could always depend on him, especially when others folded like intricate origami constructs.

At a co-presentation at a neighboring retirement community forum, Len resorted to a technique later utilized effectively by conservative outlets. He quoted directly from those he meant to discredit. In celebration of Patriots Day and Constitution Day, we spoke to an attentive audience of several hundred.

Residents of that affluent retirement community were accustomed to seeing us in dinner theater musical murder mysteries. This gave them another insight into people they already knew. For us, it was a chance to stage a presentation rather than a performance. Both required preparation and rehearsal.

Len tried for the fifteen years we spent near the border in Arizona to alert friends and family back East to the dimensions of the problem. The growing incursions of illegals created their own problems, in addition to augmenting the threats to national security. Illegals littered the riverbeds of our seasonal rivers with ugly plastic water bottles. They decorated the desert landscape with panty-covered rape trees. Locals, law enforcement, and federal officials found corpses deserted by heartless coyotes. We saved a family abandoned by coyotes, furnishing a hot meal and contacting the Border Patrol for which the mother was grateful.

A trauma center Len needed to repair a damaged tendon in an accident got closed due to the influx of illegals. Some specialists could no longer afford to work for nothing. Illegals came without insurance and received care at the front of the line. They trespassed over ranchers and residents' homes, dismantling fences, raiding water sources, menacing locals, and spreading crime. Some of Len's new friends were ranchers. Len found government signs miles from the border warning citizens like us not to hike in certain areas like Organ Pipe. Ceding territory to cartel control sharply curtailed Len's ability to explore. The ignominious surrender of the border did not solve the problem. It made it worse. Len and I watched the West we loved disintegrate.

Len allied with local guardians of our sovereignty to participate in protests that spotlighted the incursions on the border. Talk of comprehensive immigration reform did not fool Len. He knew it meant amnesty. That meant the end of our glorious sojourn in Southern Arizona.

Most of our friends still wanted to go to Nogales until increasing coverage of murders of tourists in popular restaurants persuaded them that Len knew what he was talking about when he suggested other destinations. After fifteen years in paradise, that paradise hit the skids, and Len suggested we move to another home at a greater distance from the border.

Reported tunnels across the border alerted some of our guests to the sophisticated operations to smuggle drugs and people into the United States. Inevitably, when they returned to their East Coast homes, they returned to their bubble wrapped version of the world. They forgot all about the burgeoning catastrophe at the border. Out of sight, out of mind, for a while. Len's warnings became more difficult to ignore as the border moved to all 50 states.

It requires a special kind of intransigence to remain wedded to an untrustworthy ideology. Having been raised as a communist, I lamented the conversion of friends and family members to communist policies and slogans. America saved the world from Soviet expansion, ending the Cold War in victory. But communism merely hibernated. It never died. And now the ideology that fueled the Russian bear awoke in America. It made our idyllic life on the border untenable.

We drove to visit Jake shortly after 9/11. On the way back to Arizona, we stopped at a deli outside the eastern entrance to Yosemite for sandwiches. We hiked part way up a dome affording a magnificent panorama to feast on "America the Beautiful" and our lunch. "How could anyone want to destroy this nation?" I asked, wiping away tears of naiveté. Len explained that they did not really want what we had. They just did not want us to have it.

September 11, 2001, tied us to the world. Illegals traipsing across our neighborhood tied us to the border. As the world intruded on our serenity, we found a sanctuary of sorts in the theater. The theater stage tied us to the community. On stage, we discovered new worlds into which comedy as well as tragedy might intrude. The arts conveyed "messages" as well as respite from reality.

19

PRODUCTIONS AND IMPRESSIONS

Len encouraged me to audition for a part in a musical within a few months of arriving in Arizona. As a 55-year-old in a retirement community, I landed the leading role of ingenue in a WWI musical. He attended every rehearsal and all the performances, extolling my "talents" and meeting other members of the troupe.

A couple of plays later, the director needed a stage manager to replace her friend who booked a trip out of town. He typically opened and closed the curtains and provided the director with sandwiches with the crust cut off during lengthy rehearsals. Len confessed he had no experience and no idea what the job entailed. She said she would teach him. She never followed through.

Len consumed the books he ordered, hefty volumes from the pinnacle of the profession on Broadway. He digested what was relevant but redefined the role according to his own abilities and interests. He stage-managed 39 productions with over 300 performances.

Len performed effectively as a stage manager, receiving recognition from professional critics and appreciation from crews and casts. Directors counted on his attendance at every production meeting, audition, rehearsal, and performance. The first to arrive and the last to leave, he attended to the safety and wellbeing of all. Len's involvement netted us a new circle of friends.

My husband produced CDs with sound effects. He provided appropriate music for the half an hour that elapsed as audiences of 500 filed into their seats and moved about during 20-minute intermissions. He collaborated closely with the tech crew to provide cue sheets.

Len attended to morale, providing coffee and snacks for rehearsals and treating the cast and crew to an opening night feast. Given the large number of recovering alcoholics, he had plenty of sparkling cider along with champagne for those who could drink it. He prepared everything from sandwiches to shrimp rings to chicken wings to birthday cakes when called for to create a celebratory mood. Cast in some leading roles and some supporting character parts, I particularly enjoyed sharing this time-consuming interest with Len. After years of working in separate states, we occupied more of our time working together. We loved it.

We participated in the cold read of plays being considered for production by the community theater and a couple of private repertory groups. Len preferred to work behind the scenes, even though other members encouraged him to perform as an actor. He claimed he did not want to memorize a role, but invariably he learned everyone's part.

His professionalism attracted the attention of another community theater that recruited him to stage manage their productions. Working with several private repertory companies kept him too busy being creative to ever become bored. He once had a chance to stage-manage at a historic theater in Prescott, Arizona. With one pre-performance afternoon rehearsal possible prior to the performance, he worked seamlessly with the technician. *Bermuda Avenue Triangle* was a big hit.

Working at West Center, the largest, best equipped of the theaters Len stage-managed, he boosted morale and resolved conflicts. His interpersonal skills enabled him to salvage a couple of endangered performances. He saved the day when conflicts between the director and male lead in *Anything Goes* and between the director and musical director precipitated clashes and threats to walk out. He garnered everyone's respect by coming up with solutions. After years of teaching middle schoolers and working with teachers, he was equipped to handle the disputes of senior citizens.

Len took excellent headshots, which also contributed to the loyalty of the cast and crew. My husband and I threw ourselves into community theater, serving on the board of one, reading scripts, and working with private dinner theater troupes.

In our eventual relocation to Delaware, Len found a new theatrical home. His photographic displays turned the empty lobby of a community theater into a gallery. Actors used his headshots for professional glam shots. He refused to take money for his extra assignments to help them out. He provided play photographs for the local newspaper.

Len devoted hours of time and money to spinning paper and ink into headshot gold. How often an actor would say, "I never looked so good", and ask for copies. Len had a goal of making people look good. He took headshots and rehearsal action shots of the cast and crew to display. He granted every actor or relative of an actor's requests for copies of the photos.

Len started as a teacher and, yes, John Travolta was one of his students. He secured a signed autograph of John wishing our community theater good luck with our production of *Grease*. He never left the teaching profession behind. He started mentoring programs in Arizona and Delaware. He taught workshops on stage managing to equip new people, often young people, to take over those roles. I enrolled in one of the workshops, eager to learn from the pro.

My husband elevated assistants to co-stage managers as quickly as possible as he helped his apprentices develop their skills and confidence. He found he was stage managing five shows a year, which afforded little time off for good behavior. Finally, having entered his eighties and reprioritized his time when I received a cancer diagnosis, he retired again, putting an end to his stage-managing career.

Len found it difficult to turn down friends' requests, but offered to consult, do photography and train others. He functions as "stage manager emeritus" for those on the Board and those directors conversant with his contributions. In "Reflections on Twenty Years Behind the Curtain," he shared his story, turned out the lights, and closed the final curtain.

Len curtailed his creative work as stage manager to devote his time to my care. He takes me to dress rehearsals rather than performances when sold out audiences might jeopardize my immune-suppressed health. He arranges for me to assist him with head shots and to read the parts for actors who know in advance they will miss rehearsals. Len's continued connections and the arrangements he makes allow me to remain in contact with the behind-the-scenes comedy and drama of theater.

My husband never stops searching for ways to be a better father or grandfather. His sons love him unabashedly. As his children, they depended on him to furnish gourmet New Year's Eve dinners for the family. Typically, when they were kids, watching a great performance of a televised opera topped off the traditional dinner.

As they grew, my sons greeted the delicious aromas emanating from the kitchen with the acknowledgement that "Dad must be cooking." To this day, he prepares paella or other feasts when they visit.

My sons depend upon Len for an amalgam of advice combined with respect for their autonomy. They use him as a sounding board. They share interests and insights.

By the time our younger son arrived, it was more common for the father to participate in the birthing process. Len joined me in Lamaze exercises. He welcomed Jake with the confidence imbued by that second chance at fatherhood. As a responsible father of two, he sold his motorcycle. He welcomed his step granddaughters, raven-haired Hannah and blonde, exuberant Ellen. Introduced to the family as very little girls, they brought patent leather shoes and fancy princess-style dresses, shining tresses, and a whole wardrobe of ballet costumes and barrettes to a mostly male configuration.

Len's grandson, too, judged him a loving man. Len took him on cruises and land trips, always inviting him, never assuming or pressuring him to participate in family trips. Marc always chose to go with us, which was a blessing. When we drove across the country to Colorado and Wyoming a couple of years ago, our teenage grandson elected to ride with us rather than fly across the country with his dad. Len wanted him to experience the enormity of the country and the abundance of its farms.

We watched Marc speed up the tundra paths in Rocky Mountain National Park. He took the twisting turns up a long switchback on a one-way road with glee as the car maneuvered the sheer cliffs skirting the edge. He spied elk and deer, swift-flowing rivers, and thickly forested slopes. We took some brief hikes with less demanding elevation, reviving earlier memories of times we hiked the same trails with our young sons. Len and Marc ordered wild game in rustic restaurants perched atop the foothills. At Frontier Days in Wyoming, we took Marc to a rodeo with bull riding teams where he purchased a cowboy hat that highlighted his handsome profile.

One day, stopped for gas in Kansas, we watched a black curtain blot out the noon sky. Hurrying to the car, we drove for more than an hour through impenetrable sheets of rain and hoped to escape a threatened tornado. Len succeeded in his objectives, spending time with our grandson and introducing him to the bounty of the land. Marc loved the road trip and counted down the time until a recent trip to Cape Cod…

So many octogenarians live out their remaining years estranged from their children or distant strangers to their grandchildren. Len cultivated our sons and grandchildren during their childhood. To this day, some of my happiest moments include watching them tease each other.

Now, laugh lines crinkle Len's face, but his eyes still shine with joy when he greets his family, spots an exotic bird from a trail, or squints at the stars off a cruise ship balcony. A three-generation family vacation offers an intimation of immortality.

Len recently retrieved a photo from a family trip taken when our grandson was about eight. Our sons paddle a Tonka Truck yellow canoe across Jenny Lake against the backdrop of the mountain that leads up to Solitude Lake in the backcountry. Our sons smile. Seth's son, our grandson, beams. Secured in a life jacket, stationed between our sons, he has the time of his life. An everyday event or a once in a lifetime experience can occasion joy. A photograph or memory of that event can reprise the smile.

Those were the times that made everything else worthwhile. Saving the money to paddle through paradise turned out to be more valuable than anything else we could have purchased. How often Len's pyramid of photographs enabled me to revisit a land of eternal summer and firefly evenings that promised never to end.

Even during the dark siege of childhood, I climbed ramparts of joy to capture sunlight that streamed into my memory. I explored Eden in visits to my Aunt Gail's home. That home contained the topped table cluttered with nail polish, the pantry filled with cookies, and the garden scented with roses.

Visits to my Aunt Ann's homes echoed with her laugh, which soared like her soprano's vibrato and brought forth the esprit of a supremely happy woman. Len joined me in opting for time with her sons. Years later, he welcomed Ann's younger son's addition of twin boys, nicknamed "the little fishes," to the extended family. At the dawn of my life, when the god of trauma angrily drove his trident into the earth at my trembling feet, there were still moments of magic.

There were movies. Cousins took me from the linoleum-covered booth where we lunched on tuna fish sandwiches to watch *The Wizard of Oz*. I rejected Dorothy's conclusion that "there's no place like home." I vowed that one day I would escape the confines of Kansas. "The red shoes" captured everything I aspired to do as a dance student but never achieved.

Bambi and the other Disney classics transported me to a realm of fairytale happy endings. They rescued me from the "Grimm and Grimmer Fairy Tales" that captured my daily home life. Ambiguity and ambivalence did not attend the Saturday afternoon double-features I walked to with my sister and brother. A sleep over at a friend's house was memorable, as were the Hershey Bars I won in a series of speed-reading contests held during middle school. There were times we played with our cousins and cuddled Skippy's pups.

My penmanship collapsed under the volume of notes supplied by Miss Vinson, my social studies and English teacher. She played baseball with us after middle school sessions. I rejoiced when my English Honors teacher gave me three years of immersion in literature and elegant expression. A classmate told me to write it down when Mr. Ellwood coughed. I endured the good-natured jibes and continued to take notes at college while my classmates knitted sweaters for their boyfriends. I never knitted Len a scarf or a hat or any clothing. But more than sixty years ago, I stitched our hearts together for life. Len, my love.

20

FRIENDSHIPS THROUGH THE YEARS

Sometimes the oldest friends surpass and outlast others as best friends. My first friend was my sister. We played with dolls together. We took dance classes and did the latest steps of the Lindy and the cha-cha to Elvis and Dion, whose records we played repeatedly on a portable blue phonograph. We shared clothes and secrets. As a young adult, she lived with my family for a time before relocating back to California. An incredible aunt, Tina displayed great sensitivity to my sons.

Seth always experienced a letdown after a gala event. The day after his Bar Mitzvah she took him on a picnic to a nearby park, a place of calm with quiet woods and birdsong. She frequently traveled with us when we visited National Parks or Lake Tahoe. When either son resorted to complaints, which happened rarely, she exhorted him to cease and desist. "There is no crying in vacation land," she would cajole, or "There is no whining in Adventureland." It had the desired effect. All three of them used the same line on Seth's son whenever our grandson had had enough of a long hike. It became part of the family lore.

As adults, we traveled together with our husbands and our sons and grandchildren. As aging seniors, we share health updates, political commentary, a search for God, and appreciation of our respective husbands. In the childhood closet, I had

Tina for my cellmate. I have Len for my soulmate. My sister, my brother-in-law Jason, a thoughtful, analytical, compassionate man, and my husband remain my insider friends.

My friendships were not limited to any clique. With one junior high school friend we rode our bikes to the local library for the books that helped summer days pass in a blur of romance and adventure. With another, we put on silly shows modeled after television variety programs.

With Sarah and Frank, teenage friends, Len and I double dated, chewed gum, and blew bubbles of obscenity around the car in acts of defiance. We relished our newly discovered individuality. All four of us spent our earliest years in different boroughs of NYC where we all learned to live on the streets, unsupervised and unafraid. In our small town, we explored places to make out, reveling in the freedom cars provided.

We met again as adults after adventures that took us to very different parts of the world. Recently, we shared writings and revelations, stories about crazy things we had done, and our need to keep blazing new trails. We discovered there was more than nostalgia, however nuanced or neat, to our friendship. We had the same questions nipping at our heels. We heeded the necessity of discarding convenient or comforting platitudes. The compulsion to continue to communicate signaled that we had retrieved a friendship of value.

Sometimes you let good friends go away, only to realize decades later what you lost. Now, we reclaim them, our partners in the adolescent struggle for autonomy. We are eager to continue our long-distance reunion as aging adults.

I socialized with school friends who also got straight A's. I did not compete with them, but I cried when I got a "B" one marking period in biology. I punished myself for failing to meet expectations for perfection. So much of my identity was tied up in the grades my parents promoted. I internalized their concept of me. I was my brain and its fealty to communism.

Summers between college semesters, I worked as a secretary, taking the buses and subways across the Hudson. I explored the city, walking along avenues and streets in high-heeled shoes. Each summer I met people, some of whom became friends, to whom I learned to say goodbye without regret. One older friend I encountered was studying to be a social worker. She assured me that it was okay to find people and get close for a short period of time. A friendship did not have to last forever to be worthwhile.

I had friends at college. Unfortunately, my immersion in a stage of deep Marxist indoctrination affected my judgment. It made me a friend too intent upon proselytizing. Many of my professors befriended me, leading me to a summer job at the 42nd street library, a campus job tutoring a foreign student, and the job of secretary for the History Department my senior year.

I received several offers to do honors projects and the one I selected yielded a Woodrow Wilson fellowship. Lucky me! My husband, two years ahead of me, starred in my college years. Our circle of friends, mostly his, became ours. We sustained lifelong friendships with two of those couples, previously discussed.

College friendships centered on majors and career plans, dates and breakups, dances and parties, music and campus politicization, civil rights causes and the first anti-war teach in. We dressed up for Saturday football games. Our dates bought us corsages. We cheered our marching band, chowed down on hotdogs, and followed the clash of teams on the field. Like my girlfriends, I managed to go to many games without ever mastering the rules, the calls, or the plays. Some couples got pinned, and some got engaged. We did both. Some divorced and some died, appearing decades later in the obit section of the alumni newsletters.

Our two sets of best friends befriended each other. We all went on to graduate degrees and careers that attested to the value of the education we received at the state university. None of us came from money. None of us cared. We gathered for celebrations and for no reason at all. We visited each other as we moved across the country. All of us kept up with each other's siblings and parents and with our children. We could be busy with our lives and incommunicado for a time. But after months or longer we could see each other and pick up a conversation in the middle of a sentence. We rode saddle horses in the crescent of desert surrounding Elephant Head. We walked and talked. A simple visit to one of our homes meant taking a walk for several miles to give us a chance to catch up.

One couple preceded us by a few steps in the progression from apartment to house, having children, and juggling responsibilities. I always valued Hailey's experience. She told me what was coming and offered a much overused but, in this case, richly deserved title of role model. She made fantastic orange Bundt cakes and macaroni salad. Her husband Lee was famous for twenty-ingredient salads and French toast challah bread. We alternated visiting each other's homes every few months with their three and our two sons in tow along with boxes of desserts to get us through lunch and dinner. They were hospitable, helpful, and central to our lives.

She taught math and he practiced law into his eighties. They were hard-working people and generous friends. The other couple also exemplified the work ethic. Sam became a doctor with two degrees, dedication to research and clinical practice, an accomplished grant writer, and a consummate healer. Despite a busy schedule, he graciously accommodated every requested second long distance opinion to us and members of our family.

Daphne's professional path as a medical librarian and professor who loved to cook enabled her to participate in her husband's love of travel. Both couples visited continents and exotic locales around the world to present talks to their peers as their professional and travel interests merged.

Both Len and I had circles of work friends, fellow educators, administrators, students, and people with whom we walked our career paths. Before we welcomed children into our lives, we returned at 5 AM from parties in Bed Stuyvesant or Harlem. We rode motorcycles with another teacher who instructed Len in the art of motorcycling. We roomed with other teachers at a summer camp and at weekend retreats. We went through their divorces and remarriages, births and graduations, as we allied to "fight" battles in the thick of the educational commotion.

Len and I wrote grants and conducted research. We redesigned the curriculum and participated in school restructuring. We implemented standards and went on strikes. The two of us earned "promotions" to administration but never gave up being teachers. It was the profession I always aspired to. I loved it until enthusiasm reduced me to exhaustion and I was compelled to leave it.

I always wanted to teach high school students in New York City, and I did. Len had a distinguished career as a teacher, an instructional team leader, and as an administrator for several county offices in the state. Len and I made many friends along the way. Their photos still smile out of the yearbooks of memory.

Moving to Arizona, we met new people, some of whom became friends. It was never the same. Our old friends visited frequently, staying as long as a couple of weeks. Sometimes we all met or traveled to other places or countries. Sometimes we stayed at our house as the base of operations in Arizona, enjoying daily road trips and Len's excellent cuisine. We flew east every few months to quench our thirst for family. We flew our kids out often, introducing our grandchildren to the land of mesquite and javelinas.

Most of our new friends centered around community theater or Len's interest in the history of the West and the conditions on the border. We filled our closets with dusters, boots, jeans, and Stetsons. We adorned our albums with pictures from the Fiesta de los Vaqueros, the Tucson Rodeo, and the splintered quartz mountains surrounding our valley. We filled the niches of our stucco home with kachinas and Mexican pottery and folk art.

The most important friends we found there had fifteen years on us. He hailed from the outer boroughs with imperfect grammar and a perfect memory for his experiences in an Israeli tank brigade. He knew many who had governed Israel or played a part in its remarkable military successes. The man would give talks for hours without reference to notes or recourse to a break. He had collections of coins, weapons, stamps, and other memorabilia from all over the Middle East.

His wife survived the Holocaust. As a small blue-eyed, blond-haired child, she smuggled food in and out of the ghetto. She and her mother survived, spending years in Israel where she served in the military canine police and where they raised their children. Then they moved to Arizona, and she visited military bases, police departments, schools, and other organizations, sharing her story of the Holocaust with all who would listen.

When the husband lay dying in hospice, Len spent every day there with him.

He chided him about being "a bum from Brooklyn," which elicited a smile. Len, born in the Bronx, stayed with him until the end. The borough did not matter. Growing up in New York and love for each other, America, and Israel united them. They met our sons, sharing meals with us at our house and theirs. They always celebrated the holidays with pots of food and stories that coursed through their bloodstreams. We met their daughter and her family. We developed an extended family.

Whenever Len drove our buddy to Tombstone, we stopped at a convenience store next to a gas station to get him the old-fashioned Yoo-hoo chocolate drink he had thirsted for since his childhood. They had an outlook, a fortitude, and a faith that made them seem invincible. And for a time, they were.

Len and I were blessed to have had them as friends. Reluctantly, Len told him we were moving back east while he spent his final days in hospice. He begged us not to tell his wife. We did not until half a year later when we had to leave. We maintained contact and attended her delivery of a Shoah presentation at our son's base. We phoned every few days until she died of pancreatic cancer a couple of years ago. Her book, *Life Can Be Beautiful*, summarizes her invincible spirit.

Upon moving back to Delaware to be closer to our family and friends, we made new friends in the clubhouse activities, at the pool, and in community theater. Len and I continued our creative outlet. He stage-managed productions, served on the board, and helped select scripts and directors. In addition to traditional stage manager tasks, he recorded sound effects, provided music for intermissions and opening the house, and sometimes assisted directors in casting.

Len took photographs that turned the program and lobby into galleries of headshots and action pics. I had many opportunities to act in musicals, comedies, and dramas. Working with so many talented people provided instructive inspiration. I found it rewarding to work with my husband, who never ceased to amaze me with his creative and interpersonal skills.

A few new neighbors notable for their decency befriended us. In my Substack space I encountered enthusiastic readers. Hosts of two radio talk shows offered a forum and friendship. Most listeners who referenced my views did so in a friendly manner. Responses to a live appearance and a digital interactive panel registered as positive.

Unfortunately, the parameters of some relationships redrew themselves. Some of the ties have frayed. Vivid closeness faded, leaving pale nostalgia. Taboo subjects intruded on intimacy, suppressing spontaneity and shutting down commentary and questions. Extended family relations suffered from the self-censorship extracted as the cost of maintaining a relationship. They demanded that we self-censor. Sometimes we did. Other times we walked away emotionally.

It becomes increasingly difficult to remain close to people who insist that you conceal who you are. It hurts to talk to people who shrink from free-flowing conversation. But in some cases, our ties with each other, our sons and grandchildren could not be more tightly interwoven than a sailor's elaborate knots. That love sustains me. I focus the lens on what is meaningful and discard the complaints.

As of this writing, about to turn 82, I shall celebrate another season of changes. I feel a continuously growing appreciation for the Western Civilization that nurtured me. I have gratitude to God for the gift of life and my beloved family. Friendships need not be many. Few relationships fit the demanding definition. Colleagues, casual acquaintances, even good-time friends contribute to life. Still, the most memorable and momentous times with friends continue to be those shared with best friends, the custodians of our passage.

21

CAREER TALES AND ANECDOTES

When I taught high school history, I hurried to write a Do Now (a question for students to answer in their notebooks) on the board. I stepped to the open door to welcome them in from the hallway. One day, a student asked, "Why are you always smiling?" I replied, "I am happy to see you. If you are not here, I have no reason to be here either."

Think with a pen, I told them. Take notes during a class discussion. I developed a routine that gave students some responsibility for beginning to think about the purpose of the class without waiting for orders to be issued by the instructor. Homework should pass to the front of each row for placement on my desk at the beginning of the class. The less time wasted on routine, the more time available for instruction.

If a student needed the bathroom pass, he or she could retrieve it from my desk. Naïveté did not set my policies. I forewarned them that if the deans ever picked them up in the hallways for misbehavior or they took an inordinately long time to return, they would be denied the pass in the future. But I saw no reason to embarrass young adults by requiring a verbal request to go to the bathroom. Building mutual trust prepared them to take risks to improve their communication and critical thinking skills.

When I started teaching, the late 1960s were underway. Dress codes for teachers and students began to change and undoubtedly went too far in the pendulum swing. I started in dresses and skirts and quickly moved to jeans and fashionable miniskirts. Later I realized the importance of dressing like an adult with a clear demarcation between professionals and teenagers.

At the time, my friends and I were turning out lesson plans with reading materials on three levels of difficulty to accommodate our heterogeneous classes. One kid who commuted on the A train with me, he got on in Harlem, had to sit or sprawl across my desk to attend to his work. At a distance, he was too far physically and emotionally removed from the lesson. I never sat down anyway, so I was fine with it.

Years later, I played classical music recordings for my students while they took essay exams. I read that most surgeons wielded their scalpel to classical music while still others preferred jazz, so I introduced some jazz, too.

I worked amicably for thirteen principals in three different high schools. For the last seven years of my tenure, I served as an Assistant Principal. At any time, I could be summoned to the office of the borough superintendent or to a meeting with the State liaison at our school. There were urgent calls to the Board and scheduled meetings with a professor at City College. I organized a consortium for professional staff development with City College. Supportive principals from three other high schools sent representatives to those sessions. We advanced a consortium to share successful practices, explore innovations, and provide continuing education. I responded in Brooklyn to calls to meet with the Director of the Office of Student Affairs.

I rarely spent a full week at the school without being called away, though many extra assignments took place after the school day or on weekends. I scheduled my classes for the first or second period to avoid missing a class. I wanted to demonstrate to my department of thirty that the traditional inner city school lateness and truancy most prevalent in the earliest classes could be mitigated with effective motivation.

Given my position, I moved to more formal, yet still casual attire. Students noticed everything. One remarked, "You look really nice. You must have one of those meetings." When I started teaching, I thought uniforms were inappropriate if not downright oppressive. I thought students could better express their individuality in clothing of their choice.

I realized that the obsession with clothing, makeup, hair styles, and the focus on money that characterized the heroin years was a huge distraction. The pressure to conform to school styles levied financial demands. Costs associated with expensive designer sneakers could not be met by my students.

Part-time after school jobs usually went to defray family expenses. The students who resorted to crime imperiled their own education. Unfortunately, prison fashions of untied sneakers and pants worn below one's underwear caught on.

I talked with my classes about how fortunate they were to have choices of clothing, including more than one dress or outfit. They exercised judgment when deciding what to wear to Coney Island and what to wear to a funeral. Proper clothes, or a uniform, for a part-time job, demanded different selections than what they might wear to play basketball or attend a party. Some students regretted that they did not have to wear compulsory uniforms.

It would have saved time and money. The right uniform reinforced the place and purpose. Wardrobe choices helped instill correct behaviors. They also determined the correct level of speech for the setting. Slang in the school yard and streets, colloquial in the classroom, and formal in a job interview.

The debate over uniforms became mute once they figured out that the whole point of having school clothes in their wardrobe had been to wear what made sense. Dressing appropriately to attend school puts you in the role of a student.

A student does not turn off an alarm and "choose" whether to attend school. Ignorance fails as a sensible choice. Truancy fades as an option. To be a student, you need your tools, your backpack and notebook, pen or pencils, homework, and any other supplies required to perform your role.

I emphasized the application of what worked in daily life and at home to the school setting. As the term progressed, I emphasized the discipline employed in academia in its utility at home, at work, and in life.

I emphasized critical thinking skills as practical life skills. My students had many opportunities to apply compare and contrast, fact and opinion, cause and effect, and the like to their academic pursuits. When it came to wearing appropriate clothes, my students and I grew up together. When it came to their education, we performed our distinctive roles together. More of them arrived in class prepared and smiling right back at me.

When I started teaching, I gravitated to two departments. Social studies for my colleagues and the tumultuous political upheavals of the times, and English where I found colleagues who shared my love of literature. We had grand interdisciplinary discussions over coffee breaks in "free periods" or at lunch in the cockroach-ridden cafeteria. I welcomed their recommendations for books to read. One of my colleagues in the English department remarked that I displayed the most debased and elevated levels of speech in paragraphs of parallel construction within minutes of each other. I took that as a compliment.

Later, as an assistant Principal, I worked closely with the APs of English and Special Education. We promoted Shakespeare, poetry, monologues, and projects to splice the separate curricula to each other. Those contacts enabled me to mainstream some special education students. Their fierce determination to function on par with their heterogeneous peers elicited my admiration. Students learned to support and encourage each other. Interdisciplinary approaches injected life into what could otherwise seem stagnant or inaccessible. One aim of education I endorsed involved making the student relevant to the wider world.

Within a year or two of launching my teaching career, I incorporated Black History into American History. I used three texts for my students. A book with the original and simplified text of the Constitution helped them grasp the meaning of the powerful original language. It assisted with the reading level and historical context.

I used a book of primary source materials, *Eyewitness, the Negro in American History*, to provide additional perspectives. I assigned that book to both my sons in the belief that familiarity with Black History was part of American History they had a right to know.

The standard textbook with the chronological narrative presented an overview of domestic and foreign challenges of each presidency. The text provided overarching movements and exceptional moments that marked our trajectory as a nation. I gravitated to Dr. King's vision.

I still granted too much credibility to the residual communist version of events with which my parents raised me. Farrakhan supplanted Malcolm X in alarming developments that promoted separatism, anti-white racism, and anti-Semitism. The greatest prejudice afflicting my students was anti-intellectualism that voices of the left and right recited.

Students bullied each other for "talking white" or "trying to act white." The menacing slurs intimidated bright, conscientious students and sometimes provoked violence against them. Being black and a failure furnished the easy path to pride. I relied on Booker T. Washington and W.E.B. DuBois to counter those self-defeating substitutes for an identity that acknowledged the brain.

Caricatures and stereotypes reinforced negative images that defied the imagination and curiosity the students needed to learn.

I wrote the beliefs the KKK held about blacks on the board for them to see. Racists concluded that blacks were lazy, stupid, intellectually incapacitated, brutish, and inferior. We all agreed that such views defied common sense, the bell curve, and science. Then, I asked why any person of color would say such a thing about himself and ascribe all achievements to whites.

Too many minority students bought into the worst elements of their sub-culture. Lack of intellectual curiosity led to dependence. Disinterest and disbelief in the capacity for academic success led to incompetence and to ineligibility for employment, promotion, and advanced educational opportunities. Apathetic refusal to cultivate character caused despair, dropping out, addiction and incarceration. There was nothing racists said about blacks and Hispanics that many of the students did not say about themselves. I fought a thirty-year war against the corrupt and corrosive self-defeating thoughts circulating in my schools.

Some students, one by one, would disclose personal experiences about family, friends, classmates, or neighborhood kids who challenged them for being smart.

They needed reassurance to reaffirm their abilities and accomplishments. Dr. King lifted their inspirations and aspirations.

How ironic that the critical race theory and DEI of cultural Marxism would imprison individual identity in collective intersectionality! I like to think that our class discussions and the bonding students experienced helped vaccinate them against the woke insanity that prevailed decades later.

While still a rabid communist, I participated in a faculty-student "strike" for peace. We stupidly and selfishly encouraged students to boycott school to attend a local church for anti-Viet Nam war activities. It turned out that mostly teachers turned out. For the students, it was an excuse for truancy. It came to me that the message sent is not necessarily the one received.

Thereafter, I restricted my political protests to my time. Students needed their studies. They did not know enough about the world to dictate how it should be changed. That was also true of their arrogant teachers. Ideologues in the classroom do too little educating and too much indoctrinating. That trend grew worse, even as I emerged from my own indoctrination.

I volunteered to tutor at the Urban League Street Academy in Harlem after school. I drove up with colleagues, teachers from different departments, all young and enthusiastic. We passed Mark Rudd and his Weather Underground buddies raising hell at Columbia and thought we were part of the movement.

The academy consisted of a ground floor office with a few partitioned classrooms. Posters of Che and other revolutionary heroes decorated the dingy walls. Only an occasional "stray" student or two wandered in. Few returned. After a few weeks, I dropped out, just like the students. The storefront academy could not compete with the questionable attractions of contemporary street life.

Some students I taught have reached their 70s! A signature line in *Steel Magnolias* explains what happens when someone dies young. Annelle says of Shelby, "She will always be young. She will always be beautiful." I see their faces, I can hear some of their voices. They will always be young. They will always be beautiful.

A couple of hoodlums I did not know started to encircle me on one of the few occasions when I took the packed elevator to my fifth-floor classroom. One of my students appeared like a Canadian Mountie in a melodrama to say, "Leave her alone. She's good people."

The student body included at least one murderer. Several heavy-duty heroin dealers could afford to park their big expensive cars in a no parking zone where traffic tickets got tossed away like kindergarten demerits for tardiness. One pusher wore beaver hats and a grimace that could stop your heart.

We had thugs who slashed the tires of teachers' cars. Mindless marauders stormed the halls in weekly riots. They skipped classes to break windows, start fires, and hurl trashcans. They disrupted the cafeteria and assaulted guards and staff. They left the smell of marijuana heavy in the halls and stairwells. But mostly, we had "good people" who wanted to learn, and I was honored to teach them.

I taught in three different schools and lost students in each one. I had one student whose eyes shone with intelligence when they were not clouded with drugs. He always participated on the occasions when he came to class. He understood lessons while catching them divided by days or weeks of sparse attendance. That student died of an overdose, and I still mourn.

The boy who used to sit at my desk as the price of working fell to his death between subway cars. There were students lost to the ideological inanity of their teachers. The adviser for the Black Culture Club would not permit non-black students to join, even though that violated official board of education policy for extra-curricular activities. She planted two young men in my leadership class for the purpose of spying on me.

I suspected her of chicanery but took the kids into my care on the merits. They performed well. I elevated them to borough representatives of the student government, which I ran. At the end of the semester, they wrote me an apology. They acknowledged the easy sense of belonging that race conferred on them in the Black Culture Club that, ironically, blacklisted others who wanted to delve into that culture.

After a semester of ambiguity, they figured things out. That was a tribute to their burgeoning maturity and ethical development. They understood the basic injustice of the club's operations and its advisor. They realized that I awarded them for their merit, not for their melanin. That proved a difficult thing to grasp for many, and even for adults. I kept that letter for years. It upholds decency and reflects courage. It reminds me of all I have learned from my students. I never received a gold watch when I retired from teaching. But I had that letter...pure gold!

Throughout my career, I took graduate education classes totaling 42 credits. Sometimes a professor would ask me to teach a class, which I did. As an advocate for life-long learning, I multiplied opportunities for my department members to attend college conferences, engage in turnkey training, and combine best traditional practices with innovations.

I rejected the tendency of the educational system to "doom a program or policy to success." One year, social promotion took hold. Another year, with equal research and passion, educators rejected social promotion in favor of holding students back. Proficiency and meeting standards held sway with students held back to meet standards. Then it would flip again. Equally fervent educators demanded heterogeneous groupings one year and homogeneous ones the next.

When collaborative learning claimed its day in the Teachers College sun, its acolytes demanded it be the only pedagogical method employed in the classroom. They raged against any other methodology as undemocratic. How absurd. I used group learning to teach socialization and organizational skills. Students learned to divide and delegate discrete responsibilities, brainstorm problem-solving techniques, and foster team building skills. I refused to rely on it exclusively. Working as an individual is imperative.

The consensus that derives from group efforts can collapse into agreements better characterized as artificial and arbitrary. Pressure to conform encouraged us to replace other methods of decision making with consensus. There are times in life that demand an unequivocal "no" and others that deserve an unreserved "yes." Compromise and consensus are sometimes, but not always, appropriate.

22

DEVOTED PROFESSIONAL

There are times and circumstances that require no compromise. The collective might be comfortable with consensus, but individuals denied or destroyed by it might not be. No educational technique is a panacea. Victims of totalitarian societies attest to the coercive and soul-deadening impact of enforced consensus building. The tendency of the NYC Board of Education to subscribe to the latest mandate threatens to transform education into a cultist fad.

When exposed to educational reform movements, I involved other colleagues in the training sessions to broaden their prospective. But I never mandated endorsement. It is no surprise that many educators are going back to phonetics to teach reading, and back to multiplication tables for math.

Evidence of widespread educational malpractice helped explain why the kids' scores suffered. Educators inflated self-esteem beyond that legitimately based on incremental achievements. Trophies for everyone! Teachers erased the difference between trying and doing. The country suffers from rogue unions and entrenched bureaucrats. As a former teacher, I take educational malpractice personally.

A teacher must take a student incrementally from where he finds him to a marker of progress. The teacher who fails to effectuate improvement does not deserve the job. I often thought students would do better if I could fire half of my department of 30 and double the pay of the remaining competent and caring teachers. I observed some terrible teachers and administrators. It was my job to communicate assessments and concerns from my teachers to my principal and back.

I once saved a teacher from a terrible evaluation. He had not prepared the required written lesson plan. But careful planning was obvious from the way the lesson developed and the quantity and quality of student participation. I convinced the principal to sign off on a satisfactory evaluation.

I earned credibility by documenting and removing the license of totally unprepared, unprofessional parasites. Those teachers signed up for tenure, a paycheck, salary increases, and retirement benefits without ever having done their jobs. What a travesty!

Students who came into my classroom writing only a few brief words went on to write sentences. Those capable of writing sentences proceeded to paragraphs. Those who would speak only in a small group or to me individually were encouraged to speak in larger groups and then before the entire class. I designed situations in which prospects for success were high. Criticisms were private. Praise was public.

I compared teachers, who are academic coaches, to athletic coaches. When a coach demanded more, most kids on the team listened and made the effort. Those demands were predicated on the assumption that the athletes could deliver more. Once they understood the reasons behind the teacher's unwillingness to accept excuses, they began to apply themselves.

Then, I proudly took my accomplished students on the road, I had them conduct assembly programs, present ideas, and role play at citywide leadership conferences. They "starred" in anti-violence videos produced by the borough for other schools' consumption. They directed, produced, wrote the screenplay, and acted in the videos.

Even a group of lords of the hallways and scoundrels of the schoolyard signed up to promote a different image. My community service philanthropic project in Leadership Class was run by the students on a grant provided by a charitable foundation. My students expressed confidence in the crew of ill repute.

The infamous band turned up weekly at the local library to read their poetry to senior citizens. Their faculty adviser, a member of the English Department, was an interdisciplinary buddy. We both loved poetry and we both loved the kids.

I wanted students to work hard. They discovered that work can be fun. It can also be arduous, and sometimes I was too tough on colleagues. The kids grew accustomed to rigorous demands, but for some teachers, my demands proved unreasonable. Staff dealt with tightly scheduled due dates for projects, grants, school restructuring calendars, and curriculum reform. That was in addition to daily lesson plans, grades, meetings, and State mandated testing. My deadlines came across as too taxing. That was my mistake.

Teachers had other responsibilities, graduate school, and families. They suffered the diminishing returns caused by exhaustion. I learned to schedule breaks during retreats, giving staff time to talk, snack, take a walk, or relax before returning refreshed to the tasks at hand. I furnished coffee and pastries at departmental meetings.

I had to grasp that not everyone was willing to work himself to death. The enormous demands of teachers who care about their students increased. Burn out intensified.

Students too needed a break. Students are not meant to be sedentary. When I taught and supervised night school, additional classes held after the regular school day allowed kids to make up failed classes or accelerate. I realized that teenagers cannot sit for hours on end. I had them stand beside their desks to do some jumping jacks, stretching and breathing exercises, and just shake out their hands and feet before sitting back down to resume the lesson. I did the exercises too. Accelerated activity can assist academic achievement. It gets blood pumping to the brain. My sons and my students reinforced the message that people must move.

I learned to take advantage of experts who could give my students what I could not. When I contracted with a poet or playwright, a musician or griot, to work with my students, I participated in the workshops. I called on a healthcare worker from Columbia Presbyterian Hospital as another source of expertise. Whether my workshops were for students or staff, I relegated myself to the role of student. I tried always to do what I asked my students or colleagues to do.

I endorse a concept of leadership that breaks down artificial barriers while maintaining rational hierarchical assumptions. It shows that a teacher unafraid to take risks to learn happily reverts to the role of student. It mitigates the fear of failure that impedes success. It demonstrates lifelong learning.

Pardon me for swimming in a lake of "I" statements, but they serve a purpose for bringing professional accomplishments and stories to light. I spent many hours working alone and many working along with colleagues. I performed some solos but mostly sang in harmony (mostly) with my colleagues. The following litany of sentences gives credit to me, but the reality is more collaborative.

When state representatives of the Regents exams called, I wrote short answer multiple choice and essay exams as well as sample correct answers. At the borough superintendent's request, I wrote some curriculum for the borough. Working with the head of student affairs I headed a committee that prepared curriculum for a leadership manual used citywide. I hosted delegations of foreign faculties and international students. With my husband, Len, I designed aforementioned intervisitations between my city students and blue collar and affluent NJ students to break down barriers.

On behalf of the high school division, I represented the city at statewide educational reform retreats, learning through immersion and reporting on those experiences. I conducted panel discussions on teaming teachers with guidance counselors and teachers with deans in the classroom. With colleagues, I prepared weekend retreats for students and faculty addressing a myriad of timely topics, and probably, some passing fads.

I engaged in grant writing with some of my professional buddies, bringing in more than a million dollars in monies for school improvement and classroom outcomes. I visited administrators, teachers, and students in Philadelphia schools. Additionally, I assisted groups promoting community service learning, law related education, and transitions for junior high school pupils to high school with special summer classes. In another collaboration with my New Jersey counterpart, Len, I presented on leadership at the Gifted Child Society in New Jersey.

At any time, I had a half dozen or so tote bags, each crammed with a different project, stored in my locker. Those tote bags equated to military or business go-bags, fully equipped with the necessary documents, resources and plans, locked, loaded, and ready to go. I also had the required cabinet meetings, the specified observations of teachers, and special assignments that occupied other assistant principals.

My principals depended upon me to quell student disturbances, address legitimate and illegitimate faculty demands, and work with other administrators. I served as part of a team that had to be available at any time to put out political brush fires. We lived on emergency frequencies and rations. We learned who we could count on. I wanted colleagues, above and below me in the educational hierarchy, to be able to count on me.

At times, I taught more than the required number of classes for my administrative position, given my dedication to working with students who signed up to work with me. I also trained other teachers to assume my role. We conducted weekly sessions to develop lesson plans and address classroom management. I never stopped working. I never stopped loving my job.

I left under duress. A doctor advised me to retire. My husband and sister pressured and cajoled until I realized it was time. I never regretted the career path I selected way back in middle school. As I acclimated to our new life in Arizona, I never regretted retirement.

Several years of consulting work took me from our new home in Arizona to Virginia, Las Vegas, Atlanta, Compton, San Diego, Sacramento and Los Angeles. I worked with a school reform movement that emphasized the applicability of school skills to work and work skills to school.

I connected with the LA Sheriff's Department. That began a collaboration of several years during which I trained deputies and students in leadership skills. I addressed youth conferences sponsored by the California PAL and delivered leadership manuals for an LA Sheriff's awards program.

I spent one week in Great Bear at a camp facility in the mountains. The kids from South Central LA benefitted from the outdoor activities and leadership training provided in a rustic setting. Kids accustomed to bullets marking their neighborhood saw their first bear in the wilderness. Deputies' personal interactions guided many young Compton residents from the gang-banger path of their parents to a more promising, law-abiding future.

An exceptional highlight of my teaching career involved teaming up with law enforcement. I have always enjoyed working with the NYPD. I invited them regularly to attend my classes to discuss law related issues, police-community relations, and careers in law enforcement. The most important class discussions explored the differences between preconceived notions and more considered judgments cops and kids had of each other. Several leadership students became corrections officers, police, and detectives.

Similarly, I had a lawyer who regularly attended my classes to explore constitutional and current events cases. I worked with a professor from Syracuse on law-related education. I learned a great deal from the lawyers and police who devoted time to my classes. As an assistant principle, I facilitated the classes and weekend workshops offered by teachers involved with law education. The New York Bar Association supported some of my law-related instruction with grants. On behalf of the principal, I hosted Oprah Winfrey and Ambassador Albright when they visited leadership classes, a library seminar, and an assembly program at my school.

It was an LA sheriff's deputy who took me on that final drive from Great Bear along the California highways in a patrol car exceeding the speeding limit. With lights flashing and sirens blaring, he got me to the airport on time for my flight home. I will never forget that final sendoff. I think about those police and deputies when I read about riots and cop murders. I remember them when LA explodes in anti-law enforcement riots. For years, whenever my grandson visited, we brought boxes of Danish to the Delaware Highway Patrol and local police department to thank them. The badges they wear are badges of honor.

There were honors and some accolades along the way. I battled a nemesis or two. I made some mistakes and lost some students. In conclusion, I think I became a pretty good teacher. I always loved my special teachers. I hope some of my students remember me the same way. I was especially grateful to a VIP at a major NYC bank and a liaison with a philanthropic foundation promoting service learning for their professional and financial assistance. Their support facilitated conferences, staff development, and creative learning opportunities for my students.

When I still hid in my clothes closet, I thought surviving to age 21 was a long shot. I made it. In delivering parting shots at my parents, I found less of a need to do so. I could have gotten even and settled old scores during my professional career. How much time could I waste seeking revenge or a last chance to stand up for myself? How much energy could I dispense to snipe at my parents or my professional foes? They made me their target, but they never fired the kill shot. I did not squander anything while holding my fire.

I decided to extricate myself from the bogs and quicksand that slowed me down. I remember segments of my life; sections of sweet ripe orange removed from the peel. My students live in a selective memoir. The family I chose supplants the one I inherited.

I try to live the years after escape from the closet as a grownup. It is time. A sense of fulfillment culminates in my hope and happiness.

23

JUST DESSERTS AND MEMORIES

Due to inadequate dental hygiene and a sweet tooth, I had lots of cavities. I was lazy with my toothbrush.

I still have a sweet tooth, less indulged. But I take more precautions to limit cavities and the amount of time spent in the dentist's office. Len calculates that the hours I have spent brushing, flossing and irrigating amount to months of my life.

Our younger son took fresh vegetables, cucumber slices, carrots, and green peppers, for his school snacks. Our older boy balanced his food intake with sugary sweets and nutritious food. Because I was so skinny as a kid, I remained focused on food.

Our family meals on vacation wheels merited inclusion in the family saga. They stood out as notable because we did not have the resources to eat out often. Instead, we saved for extravagant fine dining on special occasions.

In college, my financial restraints confined me pretty much to the cafeteria. Yes, the classic institutional fare, included in the room and board costs, tasted great to me. Unlike some of my friends, I lacked the discretionary cash for meals at a local eatery or snacks at the Student Center. I used the money I earned working at the Agricultural Library for essentials like toothpaste and second-hand books.

When Len could afford to take me out to dinner, it meant a terrific diner. The owner knew all the college kids. We managed the luxury of an occasional treat, and that began my long love affair with classic diners. Many of them reliably stayed open for 24 hours or at least late into the night or early morning (before COVID). Diner menus extended longer than the Dead Sea Scrolls. They offered cuisines ranging from Italian to Greek to Jewish to "continental." Diners accommodated my favorite meal, breakfast for dinner. Generous portions accompanied reasonable prices.

Another favorite college restaurant arrived with the Hungarians who fled the Soviet crackdown on their short-lived revolution. They brought with them recipes for goulash, chicken paprikash, and dumplings. boiled beef, and homemade soups. In a corner "basement" restaurant with checked tablecloths, they served baskets of bread and plates of pickles. College professors and students on a budget discovered a culinary feast.

When our sons were young, they salivated at the commercials for fast food burgers on television. I knew they were more delicious than nutritious, and prices did add up. Instead, I prepared them homemade big burgers, sometimes letting them help stuff the ingredients into the bun. By the time the huge slab of burger, lettuce, and tomato piled high, the towering culinary wonder defied ingestion. The boys complained they could not fit their mouths around the meal. The burgers might have been too big to bite, but the boys managed. We did the same thing with the tacos they succeeded in scarfing down. Today they tease me about my economizing techniques.

When one of the boys returned from school to find delicious aromas circulating the house, he knew Dad was cooking. That worked for me. In 33 years, I never moved from competence to creativity. I was happy to pass on meal preparation to Len for the next 33 years and counting, so I confined myself to desserts.

When our grandkids were little, I conducted "baking camp." We shopped to select brownies, cookies, cake, and frosting mixes and fixings. Sometimes a special event like a birthday occasioned a deployment to our makeshift camp. Other times it was simply an activity that created chaos in the kitchen but happy faces when the goodies emerged from the oven.

They learned to wash up before cooking, break eggs mostly in bowls rather than on the floor, mix ingredients, and keep track of baking times. Like playing the board games of Boggle, Scrabble, or the dreaded Monopoly, baking camp united us for family time.

We also assembled for *Nutcracker* performances with different family members playing the piano and flute and the kids dancing different parts. They performed the parts of mice and nutcrackers. The girls were ballerinas and whirling dervishes.

We often took the grandkids to an ice cream shop, a pizzeria, or a diner. They were comfortable in an informal setting with instantaneous service. We tried to avoid testing their patience or our own. We introduced them to formal dining on cruise ships. They perched atop booster seats while our grandson was propped up in a highchair. They consumed alphabet noodles in beef consommé, salads, and entrees.

High tea with tiny sandwiches, scones heaped with whipped cream and preserves, and assorted pastries satisfied every sweet tooth. They learned to sit for more than a few minutes in their introduction to fine dining. Instead of gulping down finger food, they learned to maneuver silverware and chew with closed mouths. Hannah, Ellen, and Marc graduated from their respective diets of cheese, chicken, and French fries to more varied fare.

Conversation accompanied each course and worked out well in the years before individual phones demanded their attention. I would gladly fling all the gadgets into the sea. How often I observed whole tables of family or friends, each engaged in his own device, oblivious to the company around him. Sometimes, to my dismay, that family was my own.

I confess to an affinity for the Luddites. I concede the double-edged nature of fire and computers, nuclear energy and artificial intelligence. People decide if the purpose is a tool or weapon. I regret that reading, thinking, socializing, and active participation in the world took a hit with the advent of the computer age. Gadgets and platforms that advertise connections can deliver isolation. That explains the impetus to arrange family vacations to interact in phone-free "zones."

Cruises gave us a chance to teach our grandchildren to differentiate between free and all-inclusive in the price structure. Our grandchildren learned that the endless cones of soft serve ice cream factored into the comprehensive cost of the cruise. Another trip on the high seas, another lesson in economics. We included some "instruction" on our all-inclusive cruises. We delivered no lectures. Our grandkids could wash down everything we said with another ice cream cone.

While living in Jersey, we took our sons to our favorite Italian restaurant a few towns away. We also made reservations at a fancy place situated right off the highway where the waiters alternated serving courses with singing arias. Len and I once ate in Little Italy with friends at a famous restaurant. The waiters, more accustomed to giving orders than following them, selected our dinner courses. the menu was irrelevant.

We had no complaints, which, given the neighborhood, was a wise move. Italian food established itself as the family favorite. In deference to the digestive deficiencies of senior citizens, we replaced hot Italian sausage with sweet, but the grilled peppers and tomato sauce remained.

Our trip with friends to Paris in 1967 took us to the Tour d'Argent, a culinary icon and site of diplomatic history. Eating at the formal dining room in the del Coronado in San Diego offered that same sense of history. We shared an ornate dining room site with prominent political leaders of the past.

On vacations, we invited the kids to explore. One granddaughter, a chicken afficionado with little appetite for anything else, ate many varieties of that bird at different restaurants. Our grandson, more adventuresome, tasted wild game and liked it.

During a meal at the Mangy Moose outside the Tetons, a friend hopped up on the wooden table to regale us with a story. He related the unpredictable interactions of two cousins, one with a malady that caused him to spit and curse audibly, and the other, a funny sidekick. We dined on trout, alternating bites with laughter at our friend's tabletop antics. He inspired my sons to write and perform a song for our friend, a man with a charming Belgian accent. His wife could not persuade him to modulate his tones as other diners leaned in to hear the story. The man atop the table was customarily a quiet, unassuming gentleman who survived the Holocaust as a child, hidden by a Catholic priest.

The family friend with the Belgian accent lived to work and took pride in his ability to provide for his family. Vacations and our encouragement acted as the catalyst for this public display of epic storytelling on a stage the size of a large wooden table in a crowded restaurant.

At the Pot Belly in Three Rivers, Len discovered the best biscuits and gravy he ever encountered. At the Wawona in Yosemite, we gorged on breakfasts and dinners in the glass-enclosed, vine-decorated restaurant. We also ate at the fabled Ahwahnee where Queen Elizabeth dined. At the Monterey Sardine Factory along the California coast, the waiter introduced the boys to chilled salad forks. At the Wharf, a restaurant on a river lit up with colored lanterns, and we dined on fresh fish.

Years later, visiting Tel Aviv with friends, we found a busy cluster of outdoor restaurants serving whole fish on wooden planks lined with vegetables. In Tennessee, our sons encountered cowboy steaks and tomahawk steaks that sprawled across huge platters in Gatlinburg restaurants. Everything tasted delicious in these memorable times.

We paid close attention to the catering menus when planning two parties in New Jersey for special celebrations. We threw the first to honor our son's arrival home from an Iraqi deployment. The second followed a few years later to celebrate the spring birthdays of Len and our sons. We picked a historic restaurant to which my Auntie Gail had taken my family years before.

Len and I found it thrilling to have our grandson go to tastings and make major decisions about the meal for his Bar Mitzvah celebration.

Perhaps we ate our most extravagant meal ever in Nashville. We were guests of our sons' friend. He had frequently enjoyed our hospitality over the years and made this a chance to show his gratitude. It was a lavish affair. With a few consultations, he did the ordering. An abundance of every kind of food imaginable made its way to our table. We should have gone in togas or loose clothing with expandable waistlines.

Memorable meals included holidays with the preparation and symbolism of different dishes. The meals enlivened an extended feast whether prepared or purchased by different family members or friends hosting or attending as guests.

I never attended a Seder until Len took me from college to experience my first Jewish holidays with his family. Our sons and grandkids were well versed in the rituals of Passover. Len recorded songs by opera singers who started their careers as cantors. He prepared the soup, matzoh balls, brisket, and the side dishes, setting a beautiful table with fresh flowers on the counter.

Len always admitted that he preferred a thick slice of bread and butter to cake. He relished slicing chunks from homemade loaves and smearing on sweet butter in Eastern Europe.

The case of the incredible, shrinking loaf took place while we and our sons traveled in New Mexico. We found a French restaurant lodged in the Rocky Mountains outside Santa Fe. The food was, typically, very tasty and very expensive. The waiter served a small loaf of bread with a knife and a pat of butter. We assumed it was an individual serving. Wrong.

We requested another loaf when he arrived to bring the next course. Over raised eyebrows, he retreated to bring another, equally small loaf. Again, we cut it into crumbs and asked for more. This ensued for every course until he arrived to take the dessert order. "Do you want another loaf of bread?" he asked accusingly. I do not remember our response. I do not remember the size of the tip. Presumably it was bigger than the loaf of bread.

I never knew famine, which made me more fortunate than millions. I was nicknamed "Fossil," but I never knew starvation. As a child, I was always hungry. As an adult, I never took adequate supplies of food or labor-saving appliances for granted. I never stopped rejoicing in having a dishwasher or washing machine. I remembered what it was like to do without them.

To this day, I enjoy going to the grocery store, wondering at all that abundance. I still like stocking my pantry and refrigerator with food or buying special items for visiting family or friends. When we lived in Arizona, we took the surplus red grapefruit from our tree to the food bank and to neighbors. I associate ample food with good fortune and good times.

Typically, we packed a cooler with lunches and snacks before beginning a road trip. For subsequent meals, our sons and grandson were content with sandwiches or shakes, salads or pizzas on long drives. They never took advantage. They understood that we were not wealthy.

Our sons and grandchildren expressed gratitude for our generosity, thanking us for meals, for trips, for movies, or for an ice cream cone. Watching them enjoy themselves and knowing they elected to spend time with us made it all worthwhile. We have grown older, but we are not alone.

We escaped the solitude imposed by COVID-19 lockdowns by taking a few family road trips. We went to New England, Tennessee, and Florida in a short-term bid for family and freedom. We drove our grandson across the country to Colorado. We visited Cape Ann and Cape Cod, completing the circle intercepted by Hurricane Carol.

We have plans for our two-car convoy to drive to Hilton Head and continue our pilgrimage. You do not have to fly, drive, or cruise to book a family vacation. You can interrupt the routines of school, work, and retirement by packing everyone and a picnic lunch into the car and driving to a nearby park. Excursions into nature do not necessarily require elaborate gear or expensive reservations. You can bring a frisbee, a bat and ball, and a soccer ball.

Things can be simpler like they were when we were kids. After school or during vacations, we poured out into the streets with roller skates, a Spaulding ball, a jump rope, chalk, or a bike. We introduced our sons and grandchildren to some of those activities.

Some of the constants from our childhood have largely disappeared in more recent years. Scheduling family reunions today defies the ease with which multigenerational homes enjoyed work, leisure, and meals together. Every visit we make to each other's homes becomes a minivacation. We take walks. Sometimes their dogs walk us. We play board games. We cook, or order in, or go out to eat. We catch up on each other's activities.

We laugh at the invisible friends my sister and I invented as kids and pretend to phone them to this day. We make calls to her and her husband in California or Hawaii so they can partake in our reunions. The boys do impressions of movie stars and politicians that delight me, even though they will not always perform on command.

We continue to plan family trips for years ahead. Even with advancing age, we refuse to deviate from our routine. What is not written on the calendar tends not to happen. Len's photographs and paintings purchased as gifts hung on the walls of all our houses. Even as we live apart, frames of family reunions surround us. Most of our happiest moments surround our family. Their capacity for joy has always been the cherry on top! It seems fitting to approach the end of *Chronicles of Deplorabella* on a sweet note. Bon Appetit!

24

FALMOUTH, FULL CIRCLE

My autobiography is neither chronological nor comprehensive. It is a selected series of events, emotions, and changing perspectives. It consists of memories that captured my attention and demanded inclusion. What began as a hatred for this country changed into a patriotic love of the land, the founding documents, and a self-correcting course of history. I developed a deep affinity for all that makes America an exceptional country. Some of this ideological metamorphosis was gradual. A series of epiphanies contributed. This is a survey of that transcendence.

These chronicles call on young people fighting an uphill battle against a dysfunctional childhood. Keep fighting! It is an example of how blessed the mission of work can be. Love and rationality constitute the escape route from what is ugly to what is beautiful. You are not responsible for the conditions into which you are born. You are responsible for the circumstances of your children's births. You did not choose your family. You do not owe them blind obedience. You are entitled to exercise free will. Born into dysfunctional darkness, you can claim the light. God, your guide, points the way. Love is your walking stick. Hike the trail to freedom and faith.

I try to weave the unique and the universal into a personal story with appeal and significance to others. It is a love letter to my family, friends, and faith. My embrace of Western Civilization enriched my life with Mozart and Van Gogh, Shakespeare and Locke, Montesquieu and Pasteur. Perhaps some of my more malign moments can serve as a cautionary tale for what to avoid. I pray that my more generous and grateful moments can echo or evoke my readers' more positive reflections.

My husband, sons, and grandson and I recently completed an eight-day road trip to Cape Cod and Cape Ann. We hoped to provide them with experiences that would endear these magical monuments to summer's spectacle of sea and skies, quaint towns and inviting detours to them. It worked. The boys enjoyed a fast cruise to Nantucket Island to relish the luxury yachts moored in the harbor. The sea-ravaged paint and salt-encrusted shingles highlighted by vibrant garden blooms reminded us of Old Cape Cod. The post-COVID growth in homes resulted in a few cookie-cutter malls, but many modern mansions proved worth the glimpses through greenery-created privacy.

Provincetown, always a bohemian getaway, had grown past crowded. Some parts of the town suggested a Universal theme park despite a few strips of shallow beach and the expanses of water just beyond the Truro lighthouse and sand dunes. I could see a Hogwarts-type area with shops and apartments seeming to grow out of each other. The ambience felt both hectic and festive.

Woods Hole furnished aquarium tanks, local fish, a resident seal, and a slithery octopus. Driving through Falmouth, Len researched the street I wanted to see. The address of my relatives' beach house in Falmouth could not be located. Given the erosion of storms, the coastline changed and perhaps that address no longer existed. But my sons and grandson were supportive of Len's efforts to find the place where I spent the final summer vacation of my youth before Hurricane Carol destroyed the house and killed two aunts and three little cousins.

We crossed a bridge and parked at a location on a beach with a bay across the street. I felt that we were there, even if it was not the precise spot. I had a chance to mourn. I had grieved for 70 years. Having never been at the funerals, I never felt the finality of their deaths. I never rid myself of macabre visions or ghoulish questions about the precise moments and ways in which they died. Sometimes,

I still have the recurring nightmares of tidal waves from which I could not save them.

The time in Falmouth gave me a sense of peace. Len understood how important it was for me to mark the beauty of my aunts' and cousins' young lives and the tragedy of their deaths. Having my immediate family with me, three generations of men, comforted me. I cried and prayed. The impact proved long overdue. In enjoyed being on the Cape, even with the sadness of that dramatic event that introduced me to death in a very personal way. We celebrated our grandson's 20th birthday and his academic achievements. A summer that combined our family's hard work with play kept our promise to our kids. Their lives have overcome the suffering my parents promised and imposed on me and my brother and sister.

We avoided the beaches as though the chilly ocean temperatures did not provide reason enough to confine our swims to pools. Great white shark infestation of Cape Cod coastal waters resulted in many beach closings and a generalized preoccupation with danger. Shortly after the trip, another hurricane huffed and puffed up the East Coast, mandating evacuations from some North Carolina islands. Cape Cod got hit by the storm, which fortunately did not bring overwhelming destruction with the frenzied wind and waters that smacked the area.

We had great fortune in scheduling the week we did to overindulge in lobster, prize-winning chowders, and bisques that every restaurant assured us delivered the prize-winning exemplars of the traditional soups. Balmy temperatures rewarded our explorations. Hurricanes had not yet started their treacherous assault on the coastline. A perfect week greeted us. It mirrored the one I experienced in Falmouth 71 years before. Falmouth, full circle.

On Cape Ann, Len took the photo of the Fishermen's Memorial that he had taken when he was ten, visiting the area with his parents. The old red barn building on the pier in Rockport still stands. The boutiques and galleries alternated with seafood restaurants. We made a mandatory stop at the Hammond Castle Museum in Gloucester.

Located on a rocky point, it featured coats of arms, somewhere between six and twelve floors of soaring towers with small, elongated windows at the top. The castle stood adorned with a drawbridge, a moat, gardens, a courtyard, ramparts, and turrets. It overlooked the ocean with a small island just off the point. Waves lashed the rocks, and they crested and cast a veil of shimmering white over the glass-green waters. We walked for some miles along the Gloucester coasts, past the memorial with the names of thousands of intrepid fishermen who went down in the sea.

At Stage Fort Park, we read the inscription to Plymouth Rock. We observed a couple of wetsuit-clad swimmers just off the rocks and stared at the sea. Locals arrived equipped with picnic coolers to enjoy the afternoon with their families.

We explored more history at the Corwin Witch House in Salem. The town is a living monument to an historic case of mass hysteria in 1692 and 1693 when authorities executed twenty people for witchcraft, including six men. At least five additional people accused died in jail.

Many of the stores cater to the witch obsession with costumes and coven memorabilia. People in costumes for the visit, or perhaps, as part of their "lifestyle," paraded through the town with face piercings, dyed hair, black witch garb, and curses at the ready. We observed many pets. I have never trusted dogs, or male politicians, for that matter, who appear better groomed and coiffed than I. Seth befriended every friendly dog on route.

On the final day, our older son and grandson made for Mystic to visit old colleagues and friends from internship days. Our son Jake drove Len and me around Marblehead. Plaques marking historic houses dated back to the 1720s. Intermittent thunder persuaded us not to drive up Burial Hill to view the historic narrative provided by the details on the headstones.

We did get a sense of the surrounding towns, Beverly, Peabody and Marblehead itself. Affluent homes of many different styles indicated a choice Boston suburb. We felt surprised that the roads were in poor condition. Despite the potholes, bumps and dips, we managed to enjoy visiting a town where cousins lived decades earlier. One cousin is gone now. Remembering our reunions made me smile. As a character in *Steel Magnolias* put it, "laughter through tears is my favorite emotion."

Driving home, Len decided to avoid rush hour traffic in New Jersey by visiting some old sites, including the house in which we had lived for 27 years. It is now 27 years since we moved, first to Arizona and then to Delaware. They say, "you can't go home again." We did, but I would not have recognized it. The house seemed smaller with every visit we made over the years. The renovating face lift of new shingles and paint, combined with the removal of plants, made the house barely recognizable.

We took 9W through Alpine in what might have been our most recent "final farewell." The homes built on cliffs seemed so steep that sleepwalkers could not live in them. We dipped into Alpine and Cresskill, towns that erupted years ago with big money and big lots. There are few developments. Every home revealed itself a distinctive castle. I was one of many commuters to NYC when we had lived in Jersey many years earlier. We visited our old house and the surrounding neighborhoods.

Len kindly took a turn to visit another house...the house in which much of the horror I described earlier took place. The place stood for well over a hundred years. It is small. It is eerie.

We drove through yet another North Jersey town, we took in how much the trees in the surrounding towns have grown during the time we lived elsewhere. At the Jewish Community Center, we saw the signs welcoming home an American hostage released after more than a year. Both my sons attended day camp there. Later, my older son and I worked at the camp. Blocked-off areas at the JCC reflected changes that necessitated important security measures. It is sad that the sense of freedom and informality is a casualty of our times.

We had many fond memories of camp activities and the basketball team on which our younger son played.

We grabbed our last meal on the road at a tavern that Len, Jake, and I had all visited on separate occasions going back about 70 years for me. The tavern doubled as a pizzeria. We would all go there for a treat after a day trip to Lake Sebago on rare occasions when our cousin was allowed to visit us, given the rift between our mothers. Full circle. Another firefly summer. Memories chewed over with every morsel.

Hurricane Carol intruded on my childhood and much of my life. At long last, Len and I succeeded in salvaging Falmouth for our family. This was an important trip for us. It linked my sons to my legacy and left them with added compassion for me and a celebration of family reunion. What I did in showing them my past reinforced what they did for me in guiding me to the present and future.

I hope that these chronicles remind you of all that is worth celebrating. That is my gift to you.

ACKNOWLEDGEMENTS

Thank you to all those who played a special role in my life.

My story owes its publication to an infinitely supportive younger son. My life owes its happy final chapters to the loving husband, two determined sons, and a beloved grandson who helped me overcome challenges. They restored me to my legacy by encouraging my transformation from a traumatized youth to an optimistic senior citizen. I escaped the trauma of a dysfunctional family and the indoctrination of a dystopian totalitarian ideology.

I dedicated myself to Western Civilization, the Judeo-Christian heritage, and an exceptional constitutional republic, America. In telling my story, I hope that others similarly wounded can heal and harvest the joys and blessings of each new day.

READ MORE

A poetry book by Deplorabella slated for publication in 2026

ABOUT THE AUTHOR

Deplorabella hails from New York City. After 15 years in the Arizona desert, her time back on the East Coast adds to a life of stories, lessons, and reflections. She treasures her family and friends. She embraces all of her travel, theater, and writing experiences. Deplorabella is an educator, administrator, consultant, actress, singer, public speaker, poet, wife, mother, grandmother, sister, voracious reader, explorer, leadership trainer, lover of many music genres, and champion of Western Civilization.

Raised as a red diaper baby, Deplorabella's parents shut her off from a normal childhood. A dysfunctional family subjected her and her siblings to abuse and indoctrination. She never thought she would survive to age 21. A childhood catastrophe, Hurricane Carol, destroyed prospects of sanctuary from Stalinist parents with extended family who perished in the storm. The events of 9/11 accelerated Deplorabella's alienation from the last vestiges of communist upbringing as illusions imploded. Liberty, faith, and appreciation for all the true joys of living took center stage, and she carries them with her wherever she goes.

Deplorabella recalibrated the balance between despair and hope, failures and achievements, to quit the darkness for the light. She realized belatedly that she could stop beating herself up about her childhood many years after her parents lost their authority and ability to beat her themselves. Death and evil are part of life but not the totality. The positives clearly outweigh the negatives, and

Deplorabella's journey continues...

www.ingramcontent.com/pod-product-compliance
Lightning Source LLC
Chambersburg PA
CBHW020247010526
44107CB00002B/145